D0214527

PR
605
.W3
S3
1976

Scannell, Vernon

Not without glory

DATE DUE

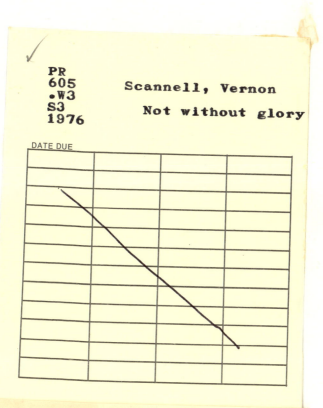

COLLEGE OF MARIN LIBRARY
COLLEGE AVENUE
KENTFIELD, CA 94904

NOT WITHOUT GLORY

Poets of the Second World War

NOT WITHOUT GLORY

Poets of the Second World War

VERNON SCANNELL

THE WOBURN PRESS – LONDON

First published in Great Britain in 1976 by
THE WOBURN PRESS
67 Great Russell Street, London, WC1B 3BT

Copyright © 1976 Vernon Scannell

ISBN 0 7130 0094 5

*All rights reserved. No part of this book may be reproduced
in any form or by any means, electronic, mechanical, photo-
copying, recording or otherwise, without the prior permission
of the Woburn Press Ltd. in writing*

Printed in Great Britain by
Unwin Brothers Limited

Contents

Setting the Scene

Poets from Homer and Virgil to Tennyson and Hardy have written much about armed conflict on land and sea but it was not until the end of the First World War that the term War Poetry was used to describe not merely that verse which took war as its subject but a kind of poetry which had not been written before, a literature which did not celebrate the martial virtues but one which was created by those who had endured battle and described in exact and often brutal terms just what it was like to be a fighting man in the first Great War of the twentieth century. The poets in uniform were, of course, all young and the experience of combat seemed in most cases to force on them a rapid early maturing as both men and as poets. This was hardly surprising. For the first time in history men, who were neither professional soldiers nor often temperamentally or physically equipped for the role, were plunged in their thousands into the maelstrom of total war. Once the effects of the first shock had been at least partly absorbed the poets who had been lucky enough physically to survive were confronted by the task of adapting themselves to the new conditions of existence as both human beings and as artists. It could not have been easy for them.

During the years immediately preceding the First World War popular preferences in poetry among the educated middle classes in Britain were more misguided than ever before or since. In 1913 *The Journal of Education* held a plebiscite to try to

7

establish the names of the most popular poets writing at that time and the results showed Kipling as the leader with William Watson, Robert Bridges and Alfred Noyes as runners-up; and this was when Thomas Hardy was at the height of his powers as a poet, W. B. Yeats was fast approaching his maturity, Ezra Pound had published three collections of verse and the Imagist movement was well under way. Sir Henry Newbolt was regarded as a major poet and a collection of huffing patriotic verses published by him at the outbreak of the war sold 70,000 copies within a few months. In this literary climate it is not surprising that the first poems to be written by men who answered the call to arms bore little relation to the realities they were attempting to confront and the inadequacy of their responses to events was often increased by their political *naïveté* and understandable ignorance of the dreadful experiences which lay before them.

C. K. Stead in his perceptive book, *The New Poetic*,[1] has clearly shown that, contrary to current orthodox opinion, the Georgian movement was not conservative, timid and evasive of external reality but, at its best, direct, eschewing generalisation and inflated rhetoric and striving to employ the cadences of common speech, and it was the example of the more gifted Georgians, W. W. Gibson, Harold Monro, W. H. Davies and D. H. Lawrence (who, like it or not, *was* a Georgian and a regular contributor to the *Georgian Anthologies*) which pointed the way towards a style that could contain the violent challenge of war experience and was of direct help to both Sassoon and Owen, either of whom could be considered the archetypal War Poet. They were both handsome and gallant officers, decorated for bravery. Neither showed great poetic gifts until he saw military action. The transformation from, in the one case, mild amateur poetaster of rural England and, in the other, insipid romantic pasticheur, into unflinchingly truthful witnesses of the worst horrors of modern war was extraordinarily rapid and complete and, while neither was notably exploratory or original in technique (apart from Owen's use of the pararhyme or consonantal end-rhyme), each developed a style which permitted him to give full expression to his deepest thoughts and feelings about the war.

Wilfred Owen is now regarded as pre-eminent among poets

of the First World War; as long ago as 1921 Middleton Murry[2] was referring to him as 'the greatest poet of the war' and even 'the only poet of the war' and much more recently and with even more critical recklessness C. Day Lewis, in his Introduction to *The Collected Poems of Wilfred Owen* (1963), speaks of Owen's work as '. . . probably the greatest poems about war in our literature'. Almost the sole dissenting voice is that of W. B. Yeats and I do feel that his famous or infamous remarks when he was defending his omission of Owen from *The Oxford Book of Modern Verse* require a more reasoned answer than the muffled roars of outrage that usually proceed from Owen's admirers. In a letter to Dorothy Wellesley (December 21, 1936) Yeats wrote:[3] 'When I excluded Wilfred Owen, whom I consider unworthy of the poets' corner of a country newspaper, I did not know I was excluding a revered sandwich-board man of the revolution, and that somebody had put his worst and most famous poem in a glass case in the British Museum— however, if I had known it, I would have excluded him just the same. He is all blood, dirt and sucked sugar-stick (look at the selection in *Faber's Anthology*—he calls poets "bards", a girl a "maid", and talks about "Titanic wars"). There is every excuse for him, but none for those who like him.'

Of course, Yeats is overstating his case grotesquely but when he speaks of 'blood, dirt and sucked sugar-stick' he points to, albeit with exaggerated and offensive emphasis, a real weakness in much of Owen's poetry and one furthermore which has been mistaken by some critics for a strength. John H. Johnston has written:[4]

'The "blood and dirt" or experiential element, Yeats implies, could hardly be combined in a poetically palatable manner with the sucked sugar-stick of "Poetry". Yet if we drop the metaphor and its distracting associations, we may see that Owen's combination of the two is a significant aspect of his achievement and one which illustrates both his keen awareness of transition and his ability to incorporate its meaning into the substance of his poetry. For those who are also conscious of that transition, one of the most poignant effects of the poetry of World War I is created by his use of the

romantic idiom to suggest, by contrast or default, what it
could no longer express . . .'

Yeats, of course, did not mean by 'sucked sugar-stick'
'poetry' or even 'the romantic idiom'. He meant a lush and
over-sweet sensuousness, a flatulent rhetoric that in Owen's
weaker poems does not mix at all well with the 'blood and
dirt' of his subject-matter.

Day Lewis, too, admires the '. . . blending of harsh realism
with a sensuousness unatrophied by the horrors from which
they flowered' but it is just this mixture of Keatsian sensuousness
of language with attempted realism that causes his worst
poems to founder. In *Greater Love,* for example, the 'stained
stones kissed by the English dead' and the pale hands 'which
trail / Your cross through flame and hail' do not convey much
idea of what it must have been like to fight in the mud of no-
man's land, and the attempted blending of the romantic with
harsh reality in *Apologia Pro Poemate Meo* results in a mish-mash
of fustian and bathos.

> I have made fellowships—
> Untold of happy lovers in old song.
> For love is not the binding of fair lips
> With the soft silk of eyes that look and long,
>
> By Joy, whose ribbon slips,—
> But wound with war's hard wire whose stakes
>   are strong;
> Bound with the bandage of the arm that drips;
> Knit in the webbing of the rifle thong.

I find myself, too, in at least partial agreement with Yeats's
strictures on *Strange Meeting* where the language often seems
strained and the effort to sustain the pattern of pararhymes
causes a good deal of odd phrasing.

> Courage was mine, and I had mystery,
> Wisdom was mine, and I had mastery:
> To miss the march of this retreating world
> Into vain citadels that are not walled.

And this sort of thing might have been written by any young romantic versifier of the time:

> I went hunting wild
> After the wildest beauty in the world,
> Which lies not calm in eyes, or braided hair,
> But mocks the steady running of the hour,
> And if it grieves, grieves richlier than here.

I do not wish to suggest that I regard Owen as anything but a fine poet when he is at his best but I do believe that the extent of his achievement has been uncritically over-rated by his admirers. Nevertheless, when one takes into account the fact that he was only twenty-five years of age when he was killed and that there was nothing in the verse he wrote as a civilian to give the slightest clue of what was to come, poems of the quality of *Exposure, Spring Offensive, Dulce Et Decorum Est, Futility,* and *Insensibility* are of truly extraordinary quality and will remain secure as a part of the permanent literature of war.

Wilfred Owen met Siegfried Sassoon when they were both patients at the Craiglockhart War Hospital near Edinburgh, and the older poet exercised over Owen a powerful and perhaps deleterious influence if we are to judge by the younger man's attempts to write in the satirical vernacular in the Sassoon manner, attempts such as *The Dead-Beat* and *Inspection,* though Sassoon's comparative chastity of language and accuracy of observation, his concreteness and refusal to generalise, must have served as a valuable example.

Sassoon has, in recent years, received rather less critical acclaim than Owen but his protest against the tragic waste and suffering of the war was in its own way quite as powerful and deeply informed by pity as Owen's. While it is possibly true that in certain individual poems Owen attains to heights beyond the reach of Sassoon, it is important to read the latter in quantity when the cumulative force of the war poems gathers strength and finally becomes almost overwhelming. Because of this Sassoon suffers by being anthologised and it is easy to get the impression of a lightweight satirical writer through such limited

selections of his work, whereas Owen gains by having his half
dozen or so best poems isolated from his flawed or slighter work.

Siegfried Sassoon was not an experimental or innovatory poet
but it is easy now to overlook how fresh and unnervingly
modern he seemed in 1917 and 1918 when *The Old Huntsman* and
Counter-Attack were first published. He wrote with a directness
that could shock many readers whose taste had been formed by
the popular public poetry of Watson, Newbolt and Noyes. In
his poem, *They*, he begins:

> The Bishop tells us: 'When the boys come back
> 'They will not be the same; for they'll have
> > fought
> 'In a just cause: they lead the last attack
> 'On Anti-Christ; their comrades' blood has
> > bought
> 'New right to breed an honourable race,
> 'They have challenged Death and dared him
> > face to face.'

Then he gives the reply of the soldiers who have returned from
the war and who agree that 'We're none of us the same' and they
go on to list the ways in which they have changed: blindness,
amputations, chronic and probably lethal illness caused by
wounds; and then the poem ends:

> 'And Bert's gone syphilitic: you'll not find
> 'A chap who's served that hasn't found some
> > change.'
> And the Bishop said: 'The ways of God are
> > strange!'

Edmund Blunden[5] has said that Sassoon's experience of battle
fundamentally changed his style of writing and caused him to
acquire a linguistic strength and economy that he had not
formerly possessed. But the quality of his work was not at first

appreciated by everyone. When Blunden showed a copy of *They* to a friend of his, an eminent civil servant and a man of some culture, the poem was received with horrified disbelief: 'Bert's gone syphilitic! That's not poetry!'

The effect of Sassoon's descriptive writing has not diminished with the passage of time. This account of the trenches from *Counter-Attack* still posseses a nightmarish, Goya-like power to haunt:

> The place was rotten with dead; green clumsy
> legs
> High-booted, sprawled and grovelled along
> the saps;
> And trunks, face downward, in the sucking
> mud,
> Wallowed like trodden sandbags loosely filled;
> And naked sodden buttocks, mats of hair,
> Bulged, clotted heads slept in the plastering
> slime.

Sassoon's satirical and descriptive gifts are enriched by a ubiquitous compassion for the victims of war and one repeatedly encounters in the poems expressions of a sense of guilt at having survived when so many of his comrades have been killed. I cannot think of any poem of Sassoon's where his grief and pity slop over into sentimentality and, unlike Owen, his pervasive sense of compassion never wobbles towards self-pity, leashed as it is by a steely irony and cauterising wit.

If Owen and Sassoon are the archetypal war poets this does not mean that they were the only ones to produce work of enduring distinction. Jon Silkin[6] makes out a persuasive case for a higher estimation of Isaac Rosenberg than this brilliant young poet and painter, who was killed in action in 1918, usually receives, and Edmund Blunden, Herbert Read, Robert Graves and Charles Sorley all wrote memorably from their experience of the trenches. Edgell Rickword seems to me a much underrated poet of the First World War and David Jones's *In Parenthesis,* written some time after the war and not published until 1937, is probably the most impressive single work to be written about that conflict.

During the years between 1918 and 1939 the Great War rooted itself in the imaginative consciousness of Europe as a powerfully mythopoeic historical event and, even for a generation which was not born until the very end or even just after the war and whose knowledge was necessarily vicarious, it became a poignant myth, incorporating the oppositions of human folly and heroism, glory and waste, sacrifice and terror, seen against the background of the torn and cratered landscape of Flanders, and the War Poet was at once a propagator of the myth and one of its creatures, as much a part of the furniture of Armageddon as trench, dug-out, Very-light, barbed wire, poppy, whizzbang, Old Bill and the Angel of Mons. So, when quite early in the Second World War, the British popular press demanded 'Where are our War Poets?' the question carried a note of rebuke as if those literate members of the armed forces who might be expected to write poems were guilty, in remaining silent, of a serious dereliction of duty. After 1918 it was impossible for the British reading public to think of a war without its War Poets.

The situation for the poet in the United States at the outbreak of the Second World War was quite different from that of his British counterpart. There had been no established tradition of American War Poetry produced by writers serving in the 1914–18 conflict and, because the United States Forces had entered the arena comparatively late, in the last year of the First World War, the men who fought were not exposed to the same long and bitter processes of disillusionment and exhaustion that their allies had been forced to endure. Although, inevitably, many individuals experienced suffering, deprivation, terror and death, the main impetus which carried the American forces onward was one of triumph, even of exhilaration. The Great War was not, for those who fought under the Stars and Stripes, a war of attrition, of prolonged and almost intolerable anguish, of the brutal shattering of ideals, but a splendid surging forward to assured victory.

A few poems were, of course, written by American servicemen during the First World War but not many of these are now memorable and there was not a sufficiently substantial body of such work to serve as a guide or warning to the American poets who found themselves in uniform after Pearl Harbour. It is also true to say that the great diversity of American poetry around the turn of the century was unlikely to help the poets of the First World War battlefields in their forging of a style to contend with the unprecedented experiences of modern warfare, and this diversity was a consequence of the role forced upon the poet in a society that was still basically a pioneering one where the artist's status was, at best, uncertain and where the 'educated' public would still turn to Europe for its cultural sustenance.

By the 1940s, however, this odd cultural xenophilia or suspicious rejection of the domestic product had long since given way to a healthier attitude among the American public towards the artistic offerings of its own country and a poetry that was clearly American, yet able to draw upon European influences, had been solidly established. The best American poetry of the Second World War—the work, for example, of Randall Jarrell, Louis Simpson, Richard Wilbur and the unjustly neglected Lincoln Kirstein—shares certain qualities with its British counterpart but there are marked differences in texture and tone which I shall be examining in the section of this book dealing with American poetry of the Second World War.

The notion that from the First World War came a wealth of fine poetry and from the Second little of any merit is still extraordinarily widespread, even among educated people, and this despite the fact that Alun Lewis's *Raiders' Dawn* appeared in 1942 and *Ha! Ha! Among the Trumpets* in 1944; Sidney Keyes's *Collected Poems* were published in 1945 and Keith Douglas's prose work, *Alamein to Zem Zem,* with its supplement of fourteen desert poems in 1946. Since then Douglas's Selected and Collected Poems have appeared and the wartime poetry of such writers as Roy Fuller, Alan Ross, and Charles Causley has been available for many years, nor has it been difficult in England to come by the war poetry of the Americans Louis Simpson, Anthony Hecht, Richard Eberhart, Randall Jarrell and Karl Shapiro, so there seems little excuse for the massive public ignorance of these poets' work.

In a recent popular history of social conditions in Britain in

the Second World War the author writes:[7] '. . . there was a
dearth of inspired war poetry to compare with the writings of
Wilfred Owen and Robert Graves in the First World War.' A
partial clue to the mystery of the Second World War's invisible
poets lies in that word 'inspired' in the passage quoted above.
What the popular press and those members of the public who
were at all interested really wanted when they demanded the
whereabouts of the War Poets was the appearance of either a
Rupert Brooke or, though far less likely, a Wilfred Owen, in
other words either someone young and handsome and brimming
with patriotic fervour, or a rebellious protestant against the
suffering and futility of war, someone 'inspired'. In fact a
journalist writing under the *nom de plume* of Peterborough in the
Daily Telegraph in 1942 hailed a young officer in the Parachute
Regiment as 'the Rupert Brooke of this war' and perhaps I
should add that the expression was intended and accepted by the
young poet in question, Richard Spender, as high praise.

Spender (incidentally no relation to Stephen Spender) was
killed in Tunisia at the age of twenty-two. There is no doubt at
all that he was a very gallant officer and probably an agreeable
young man, but his poetic gifts were minimal and there is no
evidence in either his verses or his published letters of any real
interest in poetry other than his own and Rupert Brooke's,
except for a little internal evidence which suggests that he might
have had a taste for Dowson or some similar *fin de siècle* romantic.
Certainly the poems in *Laughing Blood,* the unhappily titled
volume which aroused Peterborough's admiration, are almost
absurdly bad, even for a very young writer. A few representative
lines will give the flavour:

> I am young.
> With my proud young body
> I have run over the smiling threshold of life.
> All my bright years
> I have clapped hands in the sunlight.
> I have smelt shy roses
> And the full scents of rain-kissed woods in
> > spring.

I have lain in ecstasy
Under the spell of the cool river
When the sunset carried to me the musics of
God.

That this could have been written by an educated young man (he
attended the King Edward VI School at Stratford-on-Avon and
was elected a Bracegirdle Exhibitioner in Modern History by
St. Catherine's Society, Oxford) at a time when Yeats, Eliot and
Auden were the principal influences on young poets, may now
seem surprising but the fact is that a number of servicemen with
little understanding of or talent for poetry found themselves
moved to attempt to express their loneliness, fears, hopes and
regrets in verse, and it was Rupert Brooke who most often
served as their exemplar.

Had Richard Spender's work been typical of the poetry of the
Second World War the view that the poets who fought in the
trenches were immeasurably superior to those who served
between 1939 and 1945 would be irrefutable, but this was not
the case and it is my purpose in this book to justify the belief that
the poets who served in the armed forces of Britain and the
United States during the war against Hitler produced a body of
poetry which is of a very high order indeed and can compare
favourably with the best work of the Great War.

The authentic British poetry of the Second World War was not a
poetry of protest, still less was it a poetry inspired by patriotic
enthusiasm. There were no initial fervour and excitement to be
replaced by sick disillusionment as the appalling realities of
modern warfare were experienced. The serviceman of 1939–45
could not be disillusioned because he held no illusions to start
with. He was the son of the Tommy who had been promised
by Lloyd George on November 24, 1918, 'a fit country for
heroes to live in' and who had returned from the trenches to be
welcomed by unemployment, exploitation and betrayal. He was
in most cases either a conscript or a reluctant volunteer. If he
were an intellectual he would almost certainly be a Marxist or at

least sympathetic to socialism and he would be familiar with the
more accessible doctrines of Sigmund Freud. He would look at
old photographs of his father's contemporaries when they were
young and serving their country against Kaiser Bill's Germany
and he would be surprised and curiously touched by their
almost childish look of innocence and vulnerability, childish
despite the heavy moustaches they probably wore and the pipes
or cigarettes they smoked. For the volunteers of 1914 were in
fact, or so it seemed to their sons, an innocent generation in that
the majority of them accepted without question the justness or
the inevitability of the existing social order and the values upon
which that order was founded and by which it was sustained.
Patriotism, loyalty, obedience, courage, reverence for the
purity and sweetness of women and the nobility of the highly
born, faith in God and in the wisdom of the ruling classes,
contempt for shirkers, cowards and foreigners, these were the
fixed stars by which they set their course. Philip Larkin[8] has
captured this quality of innocence with beautiful economy in his
poem, *MCMXIV*, which describes

> Those long uneven lines
> Standing as patiently
> As if they were stretched outside
> The Oval or Villa Park,
> The crowns of hats, the sun
> On moustached archaic faces
> Grinning as if it were all
> An August Bank Holiday lark;

The poem goes on to select certain details from town and
country and from different social milieux, an array of mundane
yet oddly sacred objects which brings the period into sharp
focus. Then it ends:

> Never such innocence,
> Never before or since,
> As changed itself to past
> Without a word—the men

Leaving the gardens tidy,
The thousands of marriages
Lasting a little while longer:
Never such innocence again.

The young servicemen of 1939 possessed no such innocence. They had been taught to question the values of their fathers' generation. They knew that patriotism was often a disguise for self-interest, that loyalty and obedience could be used as manacles on the limbs of the oppressed, that women were as various and as animal in their nature as were men, that God was on the side of the big battalions, that most politicians were more or less dishonest and that the bemedalled hero might perform the deeds which earned him his decorations precisely because he was a homicidal psychopath. And yet they knew that the war against Hitler was—if the phrase has any meaning at all—a 'just war' and it had to be fought to the end at whatever personal and national cost. Therefore the common mood found everywhere among the armed forces in Britain was one of dour resolution, sceptical, lugubrious, resigned. There were, of course, a few young men who went to war in a spirit of adventure not so different, perhaps, from the sense of release and exhilaration experienced by their fathers, 'as swimmers into cleanness leaping', but these were generally very young and not intelligent enough to grasp the full political and historical significance of what was happening, and while they were no doubt brave and efficient in their military rôles there were not sufficient of them to change or temper the pervasive cold mist of disenchantment and 'browned-offness' that enveloped every military station, camp and barracks. The most popular tunes were not jaunty, impudent or defiant. They were sad nostalgic longings for peace and domesticity—*When the lights go on again | All over the World*—or celebrations of snatched moments of reunion, passion and tenderness with a loved one before returning to the grim norm of wartime existence, to the boredom, drabness and danger—*I never said thanks for that lovely week end | Those two days in heaven you helped me to spend*. In their very different ways the poetry of Henry Reed, Roy Fuller and Alun Lewis reflected the predicament of the civilian in uniform who is struggling to retain something of his sense of identity and individuality, something of his independence and sensitivity while performing his necessary function in the vast, mindless and destructive machine of which he had been forced to become a part.

If the poet in uniform was going to register in his work the changes that occurred in the *Zeitgeist* since 1914, and he could scarcely do otherwise, it ought to have been obvious that, in 1939 or 1940, he would not be writing the same kind of poetry as the young soldier-poets were producing at the outbreak of the First World War. Furthermore there had been great changes in the literary climate: of the Great War poets only Sassoon and Owen had exercised any influence over the young poets of the thirties and this was very slight when compared with the powerful effects of the work in both prose and verse of Eliot and Pound. English poets had become less insular and they were aware of French surrealism and German Expressionism, but ironically it was W. H. Auden, who was only thirty-two when war was declared, who probably exerted the most direct and widespread influence on the writers who were to record in verse their responses to the experience of serving in the armed forces in the Second World War, ironically because Auden spent the war years in the U.S.A., and took no active part in the conflict.

There was another important contrast between the First and Second Wars which resulted in a different kind of poetic response to each: the First World War took place in a fixed imaginative landscape. That is to say, although campaigns were fought in Italy, Mesopotamia, Bulgaria and elsewhere, it was the battlefields of Northern France and Belgium, or perhaps one should say the single archetypal battlefield that became rooted in the European imagination, the war-smashed fields of mud, barbed-wire, communication-trenches, sandbags, dugouts, the whole scene fitfully illuminated at night by flares and Very-lights and loud with the chatter of Lewis Guns and the heavier percussion of Jack Johnsons and whizz-bangs. And in truth a very large proportion of the fighting men of the First World War served and often died in just such physical conditions. Peter Porter, who was not born until 1929, has written a poem called *Somme and Flanders*[9] in which he re-creates this archetypal warscape and concludes with these two quatrains:

One image haunts us who have read of death
In Auschwitz in our time—it is just light,
Shivering men breathing rum crouch beneath
The sandbag parapet—left to right

The line goes up and over the top,
Serious in gas masks, bayonets fixed,
Slowly forward—the swearing shells have
stopped—
Somewhere ahead of them death's stopwatch
ticks.

Here is a young poet, writing almost half a century after the
Great War, which was finished long before he was born and
about which he knows only from his reading and the anecd 'es
of old men, yet he finds that the mythic No-man's Land, the
going 'over the top' with bayonets fixed, these are the images
which embody most poignantly for him the conflict of men and
nations, the wholesale slaughter of total war in our century, not
the concentration camps or the battles of the Second World War,
not Hiroshima or Nagasaki, events which one might have
thought to be more powerfully charged with menace and
terror and pity since they are so much closer to the poet's own
experience.

That the symbolic terrain of Somme and Flanders can so
tenaciously grip the imagination of a young man who has never
set eyes on it is proof, if proof were needed, of the way in which
the Great War has become a powerful myth while the Second
World War, to a succeeding generation, has never been other
than an historical event, albeit a spectacularly dramatic one with
immensely far-reaching consequences. One of the reasons why
the First World War exercised this mythopoeic power over the
British imagination is because it was a conflict waged by
soldiers, sailors and airmen, and very few civilians in the United
Kingdom experienced the ordeal of being under fire. The war
was being fought on foreign soil and the soldier-poets were
sending back their reports on experience to readers whose
imagination was free to work on the data supplied. In the
Second World War there was scarcely a civilian in Europe who

did not know what it felt like to be under a bombardment and indeed there were many in the big industrial cities of Britain who saw far more death and destruction than did many members of the Armed Forces.

The land war of 1914–18 in France and Belgium was, compared with the war of 1939–45, a static affair. The soldiers spent weeks and even months in the trenches, and the warscape I have referred to, the cratered and desolate terrain of No-man's Land, had plenty of time to fix itself permanently in the mind and in the whole consciousness of its denizens. This, as Peter Porter suggests, was the location of war in our time. The Second World War had no fixed habitation. It was a mobile war. Soldiers were not long enough in one place for a single warscape to establish itself in the imagination and memory. Even in the Western Desert, where one might have expected a sameness of surroundings, progress was fast and changes of physical detail fairly frequent. It is true that a dug-out in No-man's Land would hardly prove the ideal place for meditation and the composition of poetry, but at least there would be quite lengthy periods of inactivity when it would be possible, however difficult, to put words down on paper. The soldier in action in the Second World War quite simply did not have the opportunity to write anything at all. So it is not surprising that a good deal of the poetry written by men who had experienced combat and which takes war as its subject was written some time after the events described or, if actually produced during the war, composed by servicemen in more or less sedentary occupations.

It is therefore strange that one of the finest English poets of the Second World War—arguably the very finest—should have been a young officer who saw a great deal of action, in which he acquitted himself with considerable courage, and it is perhaps even more surprising to discover that many of his attitudes to the experience of particular battles and to the war in general were in many ways closer to those shown by the gallant young volunteers of 1914 than to those of the 'browned-off', reluctant warrior of his own time. The name of the poet was Keith Douglas and he was killed in Normandy at the age of twenty-four.

Keith Douglas

Keith Douglas was born on January 24, 1920. When he was eight years old his parents were separated and from then on he was brought up by his mother who sent him to Christ's Hospital where he began to write poetry of extraordinary accomplishment and sophistication for one so young. One of these poems, *Dejection*, was published in Geoffrey Grigson's *New Verse* when Douglas was only sixteen. He was an intelligent and highly literate boy with a gift for drawing and painting, but he was also physically tough and keen on rugger, swimming and riding.

In October 1938 he went up to Merton College, Oxford, to read English and there his tutor was another poet and Old Boy of Christ's Hospital, Edmund Blunden, and among his contemporaries were John Heath-Stubbs, Sidney Keyes and Drummond Allison. In his brief Introduction to the *Collected Poems of Keith Douglas*,[10] Edmund Blunden hints, with characteristic tact and gentleness, at the likelihood that Douglas possessed certain qualities that were not entirely admirable:

'Keith's character was, I believe, complex in the manner of many artists. Against his generosity and zest for life must be placed, if the portrait is to be (as he would have wished it to be) true to life, certain less endearing qualities—an impulsive and obstinate streak which was sometimes the despair of even his closest friends.'

Elsewhere it has been suggested that the young poet sometimes displayed an arrogance and ruthlessness in his personal
relationships that earned him disapproval, if not enmity, and
some signs of these unlikable traits are to be detected in his
prose book, *Alamein to Zem Zem*,[11] though here they are dwarfed
by the positive qualities of gaiety, courage, vision and compassion.

At the end of 1940 Keith Douglas was called up into the army
and after he had received his commission he sailed in June 1941
for the Middle East, and on arrival in Egypt he joined the
regiment he was to fight with in the desert, the Notts Sherwood
Rangers Yeomanry. From them he was posted to Divisional
Staff at the Base as officer in charge of camouflage-training and
he found there that he had virtually no work at all to do and,
as the months passed, frustration and no doubt guilt grew in
him like a malignant ulcer that would sooner or later reach
bursting point. This moment came with the battle of Alamein,
the turning-point of the war in the Middle East, which began
on October 23, 1942.

Douglas, who had been longing to get back to his regiment,
could stand inactivity no longer. On October 29 he simply got
into a truck and, in direct disobedience of orders, he drove with
his batman towards the forward area where he hoped to be able
to rejoin his comrades in action. Technically he was absent
without leave, if not a deserter, and he must be the only soldier
in the British Army, or any other Army for that matter, who
deserted in order to get into battle rather than escape from it.

When he made contact with his Commanding Officer he
found that many of the officers in his unit had been wounded
or killed and that the Colonel was so relieved at the arrival of
even a single reinforcement that any question of disciplinary
action against Douglas was brushed aside and he was given
charge of a Crusader tank and told to prepare himself and his
crew for action. He fought with the tanks right through to the
end of the North African campaign in Tunisia with only one
period of respite when he was wounded at Zem Zem in the
advance on Tripoli and sent back to a Palestinian hospital. His
regiment returned to England shortly after the Christmas of
1943 and on June 9, 1944, he was killed in Normandy.

His book, *Alamein to Zem Zem*, is a vivid account of his
experience of desert warfare in the tanks. It might not quite

rank with the classics of the First World War—Blunden's *Undertones of War*, Graves's *Goodbye to All That,* and Sassoon's *Memoirs of an Infantry Officer*, but it should not be forgotten that Douglas's book was almost a day-to-day journal written at high speed under the worst possible conditions and furthermore written by a boy in his very early twenties. Blunden's book was published in 1928 when he was thirty-two, Graves's in 1929 when he was thirty-four and Sassoon's at the age of forty-four in 1930, so these works were the fruits of long contemplation and were written in reasonable comfort and at reasonable leisure. The marvel is that Douglas could get a book written at all, let alone one of considerable merit, which after a quarter of a century since its first publication, still commands as much interest and admiration as when it was first read.

Alamein to Zem Zem is a fascinating work, partly because it gives a wholly convincing account of what it feels like to be a participant in tank battles in the Libyan desert and partly because it tells us a good deal about the curious contradictions and tensions that co-existed in the personality of its author. When gifted young poets turn to prose they often reveal far more of their private personalities than is shown from their poems, especially when, as in Douglas's book, the prose has been very hastily written. As T. S. Eliot has said in his famous essay, *Tradition and the Individual Talent*:[12] 'The progress of an artist is a continual self-sacrifice, a continual extinction of personality. . . . Poetry is not a turning loose of emotion, but an escape from emotion; it is not the expression of personality, but an escape from personality.' The more exact and exacting formality of poetry, the way that the self-imposed disciplines focus all of the poet's attention upon each unit of language, depersonalise the finished artefact whereas fairly loose discursive prose is bound, by its nature, to reveal personality. So in *Alamein to Zem Zem* we see, more clearly than we could from the poems alone, the complex character of the young poet, the frequently opposed elements of gaiety and melancholy, aestheticism and toughness, tolerance and snobbishness. His attitude to the other ranks in his squadron can be rather patronising, but it is the oddly ambivalent view he takes of his brother officers, particularly his superiors and elders, that is most interesting. This view, and its wider implications relating to his attitude to war and society in general, is expressed and clarified in some of his poems which we will examine later, but in the prose it comes across with a kind of muddled innocence and lacks the sharpening irony that informs the verse.

His admiration for the courage, insouciance and style, the dandyism of his Colonel, who is nicknamed Piccadilly Jim, is close to boyish hero-worship, and here is his description of another senior officer:

'Guy, the second in command of the regiment . . . was older than Piccadilly Jim and had been in the regiment longer, I think, than anyone. He was fantastically rich and handsome, and appeared, as indeed he was, a figure straight out of the nineteenth century. He was charming. His ideas were feudal in the best sense—he regarded everyone in the regiment as his tenants, sub-tenants, serfs, etc., and felt his responsibilities to them as a landlord. Everyone loved him and I believe pitied him a little. His slim, beautifully clad figure remained among our dirty greasy uniforms as a symbol of the regiment's former glory. He seldom, if ever, wore a beret—on this particular occasion I remember he had a flannel shirt and brown stock pinned with a gold pin, a waistcoat of some sort of yellow suede lined with sheep's wool, beautifully cut narrow trousers of fawn cavalry twill, without turn ups, and brown suede boots. On his head was a peaked cap with a chinstrap like glass, perched at a jaunty angle. His moustache was an exact replica of those worn by heroes of the Boer war, his blue eyes had a courageous twinkle, and he had the slim strong hands of a mannered horseman. He chafed at having to keep out of the enemy's range when he might have charged the guns in line, and found the matter of writing a report afterwards very tedious.'

This largely uncritical admiration for breeding, *sang froid*, the stiff upper lip, the theatrical pose and costume, the 'chivalry and stupidity' which he celebrates in his poem, *Aristocrats*, is allied to what seems an almost schoolboyish enjoyment of the excitement of combat. There is something, too, of the ruthlessness, the apparent heartlessness that many, if not all, artists to some extent possess, a quality which is in fact less ruthlessness than detachment, a suspension of involvement which is necessary if an event is to be observed clearly and objectively, an experience absorbed and transmuted into art. Here is an extract from *Alamein to Zem Zem* which reflects an attitude to war which seems, in its own way, as myopic as the flag-wagging patriotism of 1914:

'I had to wait until 1942 to go into action. I enlisted in September 1939, and during two years or so of hanging about I never lost the certainty that the experience of battle was something I must have. Whatever changes in the nature of warfare, the battlefield is the simple, central stage of the war: it is there that the interesting things happen. We talk in the evening, after fighting, about the great and rich men who cause and conduct wars. They have so many reasons of their own that they can afford to lend us some of them. There is nothing odd about their attitude. They are out for something they want, or their Governments want, and they are using us to get it for them. Anyone can understand that: there is nothing unusual or humanly exciting at that end of the war. I mean there may be things to excite financiers and parliamentarians—but not to excite a poet or a painter or a doctor.

'But it is exciting and amazing to see thousands of men, very few of whom have much idea why they are fighting, all enduring hardships, living in an unnatural, dangerous, but not wholly terrible world, having to kill and to be killed, and yet at intervals being moved by a feeling of comradeship with the men who kill them and whom they kill, because they are enduring and experiencing the same things. It is tremendously illogical—to read about it cannot convey the impression of having walked through the looking-glass which touches a man entering a battle.'

What is most striking in this passage is its complete honesty. It may be a limitation in Douglas that nowhere does he show a more than casual—and in many ways a very naïve—interest in the ideological, political and moral implications of the war, but his approach shows, behind the youthful excitement at the prospect of adventure, a deep awareness of the nature of his own genius and a refusal to adopt false attitudes. He was by no means a fool and most certainly it was neither apathy nor intellectual incapacity that prevented him from devoting time and energy to these matters. He was an artist, a poet, and it was primarily as a poet that he found the prospect of direct involvement in the fighting of a war so thrilling.

As a very young writer, a schoolboy and then an undergraduate, Keith Douglas showed that he was, without any question, a real poet. He had a native gift for the manipulation of language, a well-tuned ear for its music. He was intelligent, imaginative and extremely observant and he could bring these capabilities together and weld them into a single creative instrument. But what he lacked (though not nearly so conspicuously as most young poets) was what all youthful apprentice writers to some degree must lack, and that is subject-matter. This is not simply a question of experience but of experience which has been fully assimilated, reflected upon, tested against related experiences and completely subsumed in the consciousness. The processes of growing into and beyond adolescence are usually diffused and the significance of the situations which contribute to each stage is unlikely to be recognised until much later when temporal distance assists the clear view. To put it very simply: almost everyone who has reached the age of twenty has become aware of the basic facts of human existence: man is born of woman and has but a short time to live; love, sacred or profane, is potentially the most enriching and creative experience available to man but it can also be the most lacerating and destructive; that things are often not as they seem; that contradictions can co-exist in the same habitation which is the human imagination; that the heart has its reasons that the reason does not understand, and so on. But these things are recognised only in an abstract way. The fact of one's own mortality, for instance, is acknowledged by the reason but denied by the pulses. In ordinary circumstances it takes time for truth to be known, for the knowledge of the realities of living to become sufficiently absorbed to provide effective subject-matter for the poet. But in war, especially for the fighting men who are most directly involved, experience and its assimilation become almost simultaneous. The young poet who has hitherto been mainly interested in literature, in acquiring the skills of his trade, armed with which he will next go in search of subject-matter, finds the situation reversed. In war, life, death and love, fear and hate assume quintessential forms and he finds that it is experience which is seeking him out and demanding from him the ability to transcribe it.

Alamein to Zem Zem is a record of the immediate absorption of the experiences that, selected and distilled, were to inform the poems, and in parts it is a demonstration of the qualities that made Douglas the poet he was, but employed in a non-poetic way. Many of the things seen and the events described find their way into the poems. The accounts of the various tank engagements are written with a cool economy which, focusing sharply on physical detail, conveys the sense of actuality far more vividly than a more elaborate and metaphorical style would be likely to achieve.

In this extract Douglas's tank has travelled ahead of the remainder of his regiment and, as he climbs from low ground to the summit of a ridge, he is confronted by a German Mark III tank and he decides to take a shot at it before he is spotted and destroyed by its superior fire-power:

'As the turret swung I watched the heavy barrel moving and said, "On. Fire when you like, but hurry up." There was a long moment of silence. I remembered suddenly, this corporal is an operator, not a gunner. "It's stuck", the Corporal said, in a voice as if he could not get his breath. He looked up at me, and I thought, "I don't know if I'm flapping, but he is." "What's the matter?" I said, with agonised patience. "It's stuck, it's stuck. It won't elevate." The corporal began to heave and wrench blindly, like a man who has lost his temper. His fingers fluttered to the safety catch, flicking it on and off. That was conclusive. I said into the microphone: "Driver advance. Driver right. Speed up, speed up", and switching to the A set: "King Five, my piece of ordnance has let me down. I'm getting out. Over." "Bad luck," said Piccadilly Jim's voice. "I'm very sorry." I looked up. We were heading directly towards the German, now only fifty yards or so away. I had already heard the report of one shot, and now cried: "Driver right, RIGHT" into the mouthpiece. He continued steadily forward; I realised I was still switched to A set, shouting my agonised instructions to the whole regiment, but inaudible to the driver. I switched hastily and repeated, "Right, Right", until he obeyed and swung round. "Speed up or you'll be blown to glory", for he was grinding along in second gear. I looked at the enemy again but he had slid behind the ridge out of sight. He must have thought we were going to ram him. I was sweating and out of breath.'

This kind of writing which, without the least fuss or waste, conveys the tensions and fears and the oddly dream or nightmare-like quality of battle experience suggests that Douglas, had he lived, might have written a classic account of the Second World War in the desert. More closely related to his poetry than this kind of reportage, however, are the scenes where he evokes the desert landscape of war, the barrenness, the vastness, everywhere littered with the detritus of battle, burnt-out tanks and trucks, smashed guns, corpses, discarded weapons and equipment:

'The bodies of some Italian infantry men still lay in their weapon pits, surrounded by pitiable rubbish, picture postcards of Milan, Rome, Venice, snapshots of their families, chocolate wrappings, and hundreds of cheap cardboard cigarette packets. Amongst this litter, more suggestive of holiday makers than soldiers, there were here and there bayonets and the little tin "red devil" grenades, bombastic little crackers that will blow a man's hand off and make a noise like the crack of doom. But even these, associated with the rest of the rubbish, only looked like cutlery and cruets. The Italians lay about like trippers taken ill.'

There is something chilling about the cold accuracy of his observation but the power and precision of his description is undeniable:

'About two hundred yards from the German derelicts, which were now furiously belching inky smoke, I looked down into the face of a man lying hunched up in a pit. His expression of agony seemed so acute and urgent, his stare so wild and despairing, that for a moment I thought him alive. He was like a cleverly posed waxwork, for his position suggested a paroxysm, an orgasm of pain. He seemed to move and writhe. But he was stiff. The dust which powdered his face like an actor's lay on his wide open eyes, whose stare held my gaze like the Ancient Mariner's. He had tried to cover his wounds with towels against the flies. His haversack lay open, from which he had taken towels and dressings. His water-bottle lay tilted with the cork out. Towels and haver-sack were dark with dried blood, darker still with a great concourse of flies.'

Images from both of these prose extracts were to find their way into subsequent poems.

Naturally enough, there is not a great deal about literature and the arts in *Alamein to Zem Zem* but there is sufficient to let us know that even under the stress of action Douglas was aware of the relevance of poetry to the most extreme forms of experience. One of the first corpses he saw was that of a Libyan soldier and he was reminded—rather inappropriately, I would have thought—of Rimbaud's *Dormeur du Val*. Elsewhere he refers to Sassoon's poem, *The General*, he quotes the first stanza of Verlaine's *Chanson D'Automne* and some lines from an imagist poem by T. E. Hulme. He also mentions that he carried a Penguin edition of Shakespeare's sonnets into his first battle and the only other books he records having read are a rather odd mixture: *National Velvet, Alice in Wonderland,* a *Survey of Surrealism* (possibly by David Gascoyne, though Douglas does not say so), *Story of an African Farm* and *The Quest for Corvo*.

In fact *Alamein to Zem Zem* is, perhaps a little self-consciously, an 'unliterary' book, but that is not to say that it will not find a permanent place in the literature of modern war. It contains some unforgettable images of the desert battlefields and more powerfully than any prose work of the period that I know it gives the reader the sense of fear, exultation, fatigue and shock, the experience of action. It is also a notebook containing many of the preoccupations and images that were to appear in the poetry of a young writer whose best work, I contend, can take its place honourably beside the finest poems written in either the First or Second World Wars.

As I have remarked, Keith Douglas's earliest poetry, some of it written when he was no more than fifteen years old, is unusually accomplished, even for the most precocious young poet, and in these early poems may be discerned certain themes that were to remain of interest to the poet throughout his short life. *Mummers*, the first poem in *The Collected Poems* and written in 1934, is full of colourful imagery that is essentially theatrical; the furniture of the poem is artificial, brilliant with 'winking cups and wines', 'brighter silks', an 'ancient gargoyle, weather-addled / And striped with melted tapestry / Of snow . . .' The poems ends:

> Soon come the masked mummers, knocking
> With hands snow-red. The door's unlocking
> Answers the stars with indoor light.
> Now to the drum tap, with snow-crusted
> Cardboard steed, and ancient rusted
> Blade, the Saint and Turk will fight.

The whole thing is almost entirely decorative and of course it lacks the substance of informing experience, but the quality of the writing would not disgrace anyone and from a boy of fourteen it is not much short of amazing.

A poem written in the following year, *Famous Men,* seems to me equally remarkable for its unfussy but fastidious language:

> The air is advertised of seas
> they smote, from green to copper.
> They were merciful men.
>
> And think, like plates lie deep
> licked clean their skulls,
> rest beautifully, staring.

In *Villanelle of Gorizia*, written when he was aged seventeen, he shows how rapidly he is mastering the control of prescribed forms and how cunningly he can play rhythmic changes on a regular iambic line:

> All this the bottle says, that I have quite
> poured out. The wine slides in my throat and
> >   grieves.
> Over and over the street is repeated with
> >   sunlight,
> the flutes sound in the wineshop, out of sight.

Then, as technical skill develops, the romantic props of the very early poems are modified or discarded and he begins to write about simple experiences such as *On Leaving School*:

> One of us will be the kettle past care of
> >   tinkers,
> Rejected, one the tip-top apple, the winking
> Sun's friend. It will be that way, and Time on
> >   our ground

> Will sweep like a maid, and where we were be
> >   clean.
> Shall we find room to laugh, if turning round
> We see where we have walked, how wrong we
> >   have been?

The language here, just as in *Famous Men*, seems to owe something to the early Auden but that is of less importance than the fact that an individual note is beginning to creep into the poetry; it is a note of melancholy, an acute consciousness of time as the necessary enemy, the element in which we are consumed, yet outside of which our destiny, growth, creation and fulfilment are impossible. Along with this the grip on mundane quotidian experiences grows firmer and the more tinselly theatrical images disappear though a strongly developed dramatic sense remains. After the few poems of his juvenilia the direction of his verse is usually away from the over-decorated romantic towards a clean and exact language, sharpness of outline and the sure handling of argument without sagging into prose.

> Leo in drawing Deirdre's lips
> drew as hand and pen were sent
> by heaven. This perfection slips
> through the hand to the instrument.
>
> Expert diplomats' good taste
> the curious statement of a child
> or in his enamelled case
> the doughty beetle hard and wild.
>
> All in different degrees
> embody the celestial thing
> and the wise man will learn of these
> analysis is worshipping.
>
> (From *Extension to Francis Thompson*)

Ted Hughes, in his Introduction to the *Selected Poems*,[13] maintains that Douglas's work moved through three stages, the virtuoso juvenilia, the poetry he wrote at Oxford and the final phase the start of which was indicated by a poem he wrote, while still at the University, called *The Deceased*. Hughes writes:

'Here, the picturesque or merely decorative side of his imagery disappears; his descriptive powers, sharpen to realism. The impression is of a sudden mobilizing of the poet's will, a clearing of his vision, as if from sitting considering possibilities and impossibilities he had stood up to act. Pictures of things no longer interest him much: he wants their substance, their nature, and their consequences in life. At once, and quite suddenly, his mind is whole, as if united by action, and he produces poetry that is both original and adult. Already, in this poem "The Deceased", we can see what is most important of all about Douglas. He has not simply added poems to poetry, or evolved a sophistication. He is a renovator of language. It is not that he uses words in jolting combinations, or with titanic extravagance, or curious precision. His triumph lies in the way he renews the simplicity of ordinary talk, and he does this by infusing every word with a burning exploratory freshness of mind—partly impatience, partly exhilaration at speaking the forbidden thing, partly sheer casual ease of penetration. The music that goes along with this, the unresting variety of intonation and movement within his patterns, is the natural path of such confident, candid thinking.'

The generalisations about Douglas's are sound enough, if rather grandiloquently expressed, but I cannot agree with Hughes that there was a sudden change in his work nor that the poem, *The Deceased*, heralded this change. Certainly *The Deceased* is less ornate than some of the earlier work but it is a mannered piece of writing, very adroit but related one feels to something that he has read rather than to things seen and felt at first hand. The poem has a rather self-regarding elegance, a slightly archaic flavour the exact cause of which it is not easy to isolate but rests I think in diction and syntax, in the dandified locutions of 'I grant', 'liquored'. Here is the opening of the poem:

He was a reprobate I grant
and always liquored till his money went.

His hair depended in a noose from
a Corona Veneris. His eyes, dumb

like prisoners in their cavernous slots, were
settled in attitudes of despair.

You who God bless you never sunk so low
censure and pray for him that he was so . . .

There is a feeling about this, and a few other poems written around the same time, not so much of an involvement with seventeenth-century poetry as with much more recent verse which has taken as model a synthesis of metaphysical and restoration styles to produce a mixture of the antiquated and modern, which in the hands of a poet as gifted as John Crowe Ransom can be very attractive indeed, and which Keith Douglas handles very creditably. The poem which follows *The Deceased* in the *Collected Poems, Reproach*, is far more obviously 'literary' with its references to Ulysses, Troilus and Cressida and its Jacobean invective, and *John Anderson*, which is about a 'scholarly gentleman' who is killed in battle, has many lines which the Douglas of a couple of years later would have found affected and—again despite the ease with which he brings them off—too remote from the reality that they are supposed to be dealing with.

> John Anderson, a scholarly gentleman
> advancing with his company in the attack
> received some bullets through him as he ran.

This opening is all right, cool and understated, and it sorts well with its subject: John Anderson would have approved the scholarly and gentlemanly tone; but the man who has actually seen soldiers killed on the field of battle is unlikely to be taken with lines like these:

> But I think, the last moment of his gaze
> beheld the father of gods and men,
> Zeus, leaning from heaven as he dies,
>
> whom in his swoon he hears again
> summon Apollo in the Homeric tongue:
> Descend Phoebus and cleanse the stain
>
> of dark blood from the body of John
>   Anderson.

Give him to Death and Sleep,
who'll bear him as they can

out of the range of darts to the broad vale
of Lycia; there lay him in a deep
solemn content on some bright dale.

Keith Douglas's intention is clear and is executed with more than common skill but he is still at the stage when his poetic equipment needs to be tested on the hard rocks of some crucial experience before the superfluous, the merely showy parts of it can be discarded, and what is left perfected for its task. This is not to say that his Oxford poetry is negligible when compared with the poems of army experience and it would be foolish to attempt to separate the two. The poem called *Russians*—which Hughes surprisingly omits from the *Selected Poems*—although it has its origin in a newspaper report of Russian soldiers in the campaign against Finland being frozen to death and being found holding their rifles ready to fire, and was written at least a couple of years before Douglas himself saw active service, it does in its laconic style point forward to the tough, flexible and compressed style of the best of the desert poems.

Walk among the innocuous parade
and touch them if you like, they're properly
                                        stayed:
keep out of their line of sight and they won't
                                        look.
Think of them as waxworks, or think they're
                                        struck
with a dumb immobile spell,
to wake in a thousand years with the sweet
                                        force
of spring upon them in the merry world. Well,
at least forget what happens when it thaws.

But we are chiefly concerned here with the poems that he

wrote after he was in uniform, especially those which deal directly with his reactions to the dangers, excitements and vicissitudes, the peculiar beauty and horror of battle. Ted Hughes writes:

'In a sense, war was his ideal subject: the burning away of all human pretensions in the ray cast by death. This was the vision, the unifying generalization that shed the meaning and urgency into all his observations and particulars: not truth is beauty only, but truth kills everybody. The truth of a man is the doomed man in him or his dead body. Poem after poem circles this idea, as if his mind were tethered. At the bottom of it, perhaps, is his private muse, not a romantic symbol of danger and temptation, but the plain foreknowledge of his own rapidly-approaching end—a foreknowledge of which he becomes fully conscious in two of his finest poems.'

The sense of mortality and the paradoxical view of time as thief and donor, the sense of a man carrying his death within him, were not elements new to his Middle East poetry, they were haunting presences in the best of his undergraduate work, in poems such as *A Round Number, Time and Death* and *Time Eating*, but there is no doubt that his personal introduction to Death in the North African desert and their close familiarity throughout that campaign brought the terrible realities and ironies of the Last Enemy's power into vivid close-up and the old theatrical tricks of the earlier work ('Time and Death, villains in the wings') gave way to a harsh yet resonant celebration of Death's true principality.

I do not think there can be much doubt that Keith Douglas was haunted by a strong premonition of his own death in action. It might be objected that every man in a fighting unit at that quite early stage of the war would suffer a similar feeling of his impending and violent end, but the truth is that the majority of fighting men, while rationally conscious of the chances of their being killed in action, did not really believe that they would be chosen. They feared death, were uneasily aware that his choice of victim was random, but this is a vastly different condition from Douglas's amazingly brave, clear-sighted and unhistrionic contemplation of the inevitable.

Simplify Me When I'm Dead was written just before he went out
to the Middle East. Poor old Rupert Brooke has had enough
mud thrown at his *The Soldier*, but, quite apart from the dignity,
intelligence and economy of Douglas's poem compared with
Brooke's sentimental advertising copy for good English
fertiliser, it is instructive to note that the First World War
poet's sonnet begins with the conditional clause, 'If I should
die . . .', whereas Douglas writes '. . . when I am dead', and the
removal of any question of survival places him squarely before
the bone-hard reality of his subject.

Remember me when I am dead
and simplify me when I'm dead.

As the processes of earth
strip off the colour and the skin:
take the brown hair and blue eye

and leave me simpler than at birth,
when hairless I came howling in
as the moon entered the cold sky.

Of my skeleton perhaps,
so stripped, a learned man will say
'He was of such a type and intelligence', no
                                         more.

Thus when in a year collapse
particular memories, you may
deduce, from the long pain I bore

the opinions I held, who was my foe
and what I left, even my appearance
but incidents will be no guide.

Time's wrong-way telescope will show
a minute man ten years hence
and by distance simplified.

Through that lens see if I seem
substance or nothing: of the world
deserving mention or charitable oblivion,

not by momentary spleen
or love into decision hurled,
leisurely arrive at an opinion.

Remember me when I am dead
and simplify me when I'm dead.

The versification is unobtrusively brilliant, as are the shifting
stresses and the way the rhymes knit the stanzas together
without the slightest suggestion of strain, but it is the coolness,
the balance and restraint that I find most impressive, both
moving and a little unnerving. That a young man of twenty-one,
about to sail to Egypt to fight in a war which at that time looked
as if it would go on for many years and would probably end in
an enemy victory, that he could contemplate his own death so
calmly seems quite extraordinary, and the lack of orchestration
in the poem, the total absence of heroics, seem to me guarantees
of its honesty and seriousness.

When Douglas arrived in the Middle East he wrote a number
of poems about the exiled soldier's life in foreign cities and in
these he showed his exact painter's eye for detail, but, more
difficult to achieve, he transmits the feel of what it was like to
be an uneasy guest in an alien, suspect and suspicious land,
lonely, threatened and robbed of all the certainties and consolations of the familiar scenes of home.

Here I am a stranger clothed
in the separative glass cloak
of strangeness. The dark eyes, the bright-
                                   mouthed
smiles, glance on the glass and break
falling like fine strange insects.

But from the grass, the inexorable lizard,

the dart of hatred for all strangers finds
in this armour, proof only against friends
breach after breach, and like the gnat is busy
wounding the skin, leaving poison there.

(From Syria I)

It is noticeable that some of the poems he wrote in the Middle East before going into action at El Alamein show a lack of confidence which often betrays itself in a failure to bring works to satisfactory completion or, as in *The Knife*, a regression to the kind of over-decorative romantic imagery of his juvenilia:

Your hair explicable as a waterfall
in some black liquid cooled by legend
fell across my thought in a moment,
became a garment I am naked without,
lines drawn across through morning and
evening.

And in your body each minute I died;
moving your thigh could disinter me
from a grave in a distant city:
your breasts deserted by cloth, clothed in
twilight
filled me with tears, sweet cups of flesh.

The Offensive is weakened by the banality of its ending and in *I Listen to the Desert Wind* a fine lyric is again spoilt by the awful last line:

O turn in the dark bed again
and give to him what once was mine
and I'll turn as you turn
and kiss my swarthy mistress pain.

Egypt is an excellent piece of atmospheric observation, but it, too, is weakened at the end by a sentence of awkward social comment though *Behaviour of Fish in an Egyptian Tea Garden* makes no such mistake and is a marvellously sustained metaphor, the kind of thing that can so easily fall to pieces in less expert hands.

In *Cairo Jag* Douglas contrasts the hectic and—to the soldier on leave—the bewilderingly various and exotic life of the Egyptian capital to the desert, only a hundred miles or so away, where the war is being fought and men are dying. It begins, laconically:

> Shall I get drunk or cut myself a piece of cake,
> a pasty Syrian with a few words of English
> or the Turk who says she is a princess. . . .

Douglas then provides some accurate shots of the less salubrious parts of the city:

> But there are streets dedicated to sleep
> stenches and sour smells, the sour cries
> do not disturb their application to slumber
> all day, scattered on the pavement like rags
> afflicted with fatalism and hashish. The
> > women
> offering their children brown-paper breasts
> dry and twisted, elongated like the skull,
> Holbein's signature.

The soldier looks on the scene, sadly and wearily, the prostitutes, the beggars, the mutilated and depraved; he sees all about him dishonesty, greed and suffering. The scene again changes:

> But by a day's travelling you reach a new
> > world

the vegetation is of iron
dead tanks, gun barrels split like celery
the metal brambles have no flowers or berries
and there are all sorts of manure, you can
                                        imagine
the dead themselves, their boots, and
                                    possessions
clinging to the ground, a man with no head
has a packet of chocolate and a souvenir of
                                        Tripoli.

This poem captures the atmosphere of wartime Cairo with almost uncanny accuracy and it displays Douglas's gift for the sharp visual image which brings the furniture of both city and battlefield into razor-sharp focus. No overt comment is made, but the message is clear enough: in the foreign capital you find frustration, corruption, filth and deceit. Where can you escape to? The desert, the wilderness where only death awaits. The poem is a perfect image of modern war.

One of the distinctive things about Keith Douglas's Middle East poems is their total lack of self-pity and the absolute refusal to indulge in nostalgic evocations of the joys of civilian life, of peace, security, love and home. The best of his poetry is at once passionate and impersonal, and in poems like *Snakeskin and Stone, Dead Men,* and *Mersa* it is beguiling to watch the confident play of intelligence which is fused with a delicate sensuousness in a language that is at once crystalline and richly suggestive.

Tonight the moon inveigles them
to love: they infer from her gaze
her tacit encouragement.
Tonight the white dresses and the jasmin scent
in the streets. I in another place
see the white dresses glimmer like moths.
                                        Come

to the west, out of that trance, my heart—

here the same hours have illumined
sleepers who are condemned or reprieved
and those whom their ambitions have
                              deceived;
the dead men whom the wind
powders till they are like dolls. . . .

                              (From *Dead Men*)

Ian Hamilton, in his essay, *The Forties*,[14] surprisingly under-
values Keith Douglas, and his criticism of *Vergissmeinicht*,
Douglas's best-known and most widely anthologised poem, is
perversely dismissive. He writes that it seems '. . . rather prim
and frozen in its formality. It is shoddy in a number of key
places—"the paper eye", "burst stomach like a cave", "the
swart flies", "the entry of a demon"—and there is a constant,
debilitating pressure to make fable: the facts seem wrenched and
cerebrally reconsidered; rhyme words clot uncomfortably and
there are irritating inversions and compressions. One feels
that Douglas might have been happier had the plot been rather
less powerful, less limiting to his taste for the spectral.'

Here is the poem, *Vergissmeinicht*:

Three weeks gone and the combatants gone,
returning over the nightmare ground
we found the place again, and found
the soldier sprawling in the sun.

The frowning barrel of his gun
overshadowing. As we came on
that day, he hit my tank with one
like the entry of a demon.

Look. Here in the gunpit spoil
the dishonoured picture of his girl
who has put: *Steffi. Vergissmeinicht*
in a copybook gothic script.

We see him almost with content
abased, and seeming to have paid
and mocked at by his own equipment
that's hard and good when he's decayed.

But she would weep to see today
how on his skin the swart flies move;
the dust upon the paper eye
and the burst stomach like a cave.

For here the lover and killer are mingled
who had one body and one heart.
And death who had the soldier singled
has done the lover mortal hurt.

First, let us take Hamilton's 'prim and frozen in its formality'. One might reasonably understand this phrase to mean that the poem is composed to a prescribed form, that the metre is mechanical, the stanzas inflexible and the language commonplace. In fact the quatrains are managed with considerable craft and the rhythmic shifts in the four stress lines are artfully contrived. The first stanza is compact, the short sentence containing a great deal of necessary information, the form approximating to the stanza used by Tennyson in *In Memoriam* which is repeated in the second quatrain where the final rhyme of the first is echoed through all four lines with a feminine rhyme at the end and a counterpointed line. Then comes the arresting *Look* which insists on a dramatic pause before the essential matter of the poem is introduced. This is a key stanza. The narrator, representative of his comrades, and indeed of all soldiers, effaces himself here and we see the squalid rubbish of the deserted gunpit and among it the photograph of the dead soldier's girl, her sentimental and, in the context, bitterly ironic appeal—*Vergissmeinicht*, forget me not. The rhyme or half-rhyme pattern changes to couplets then, in the next two quatrains, as the first-person plural narrator returns, so yet a fresh order of rhymes with assonances echoing from *decayed* into the *today* and *cave* of the next unit. And so into the last moving lines which are surely faultless, irreducible.

This kind of analysis does not of course do anything to increase enjoyment or deepen understanding of a poem but I hope it does something towards showing the injustice of Hamilton's stricture. Next, he talks about the poem being 'shoddy in a number of key places' but the examples he supplies of this shoddiness seem to me evidence of Douglas's gift for the right word and the exact image. *Paper eye* is very accurate for the unwinking and glazed stare of the dead soldier; the living gleam has gone, the eye can see no more than paper can see, nor can it feel, indifferent to the dust that settles on it. *The burst stomach like a cave* does not seem to me a shoddy image. Again, it is visually sharp and accurate, the dark and uninviting mouth of the great wound is cavernous, and what Hamilton's objection to *swart flies* can be I cannot imagine. *Swart* seems a particularly good word here; it is unexpected and it carries more than the primary meaning of 'black'; even its sound and its look suggest something of its Old English meaning of 'baleful', 'malignant'. '*The entry of a demon* is perhaps more commonplace but it works well enough in context and, as for 'irritating inversions and compressions', I detect none.

Vergissmeinicht is probably not Keith Douglas's best poem but it succeeds admirably in what it sets out to do. His pity for the dead German soldier is unsentimental and the corpse is clearly seen for what it is, a lump of rapidly decaying flesh, but it also functions in the poem as an emblem for the duality of the human psyche—the lover and soldier, killer and creator—which is exaggerated by the circumstances of war. In *Vergissmeinicht*, as in quite a number of Douglas's desert poems, the presences of love and mortality harden into sexuality and death, lover and killer who can be united only in the oblivious dark.

How to Kill is a less well-known work than *Vergissmeinicht* but it is just as impressive in its more oblique treatment of similar subject-matter. It opens with a stanza which uses the image of a ball (the plaything of childhood) being thrown into the air, almost as if Douglas has taken the last two lines of Dylan Thomas's *Should Lanterns Shine* for the starting-point of his own poem, but his intention and strategy are quite different from Thomas's.

> The ball fell in my hand, it sang
> in the closed fist: *Open Open*
> *Behold a gift designed to kill.*

The second stanza begins:

> Now in my dial of glass appears
> the soldier who is going to die.

The dial of glass is the telescopic sights of the sniper and also the clairvoyant's glass which lends visionary powers to the gazer. The sniper kills his victim and reflects:

> . . . . I am amused
> to see the centre of love diffused
> and the waves of love travel into vacancy.
> How easy it is to make a ghost.

The poem ends:

> The weightless mosquito touches
> her tiny shadow on the stone,
> and with how like, how infinite
> a lightness, man and shadow meet.
> They fuse. A shadow is a man
> when the mosquito death approaches.

Man and shadow become one at the approach of the mosquito death, the mindless killer, the sniper's bullet that whines like an insect; in the midst of life we are in death is a truth which, in time of peace, may be, if not forgotten, at least comfortably shelved somewhere out of sight, but for the soldier fighting a war it is continually thrust upon him and its paradoxical implications were constantly re-explored by Douglas.

This brooding upon death was accompanied by another almost obsessive preoccupation: in battle the participants are playing for keeps; when death is the penalty for error, mis-judgement or for simply being there the soldier has no time for the striking of attitudes or displays of histrionics. His courage is authentic and pure. Ian Hamilton writes:

'Just as at Oxford he had idealized the remote aristocrats of learning, so in wartime he tends to mythologize the chivalric hero, the "scarlet and tall / Leisurely fellows" who "stroll with royal slow motion", a "gentle / obsolescent band of heroes". This attitude somewhat uncomfortably co-exists with an intermittent, and much less convincing, recognition of the physical facts:

> Peter was unfortunately killed by an 88
> it took his leg away, he died in the ambulance
> I saw him crawling on the sand; he said
> It's most unfair, they've shot my foot off.

Allowing for their attempt at a Sassoonish ironical terseness, these lines do instance a danger which Douglas did not always escape, that of reticence stiffening into the tight-lipped insensitivity of the officers' mess.'

Despite Ian Hamilton's 'allowing for . . . ironical terseness' one suspects that it is in fact the irony in *Aristocrats* (the poem from which the lines quoted come) that he has failed properly to take account of just as he does not seem aware of the ambiguity of Douglas's attitude to his 'heroes'. The epigraph to the poem, 'I think I am becoming a God', was spoken, according to Suetonius, by the Emperor Vespasian on his death bed, and its use here is surely an earnest of the poet's satirical intention. Or partly satirical. He is also, as Hamilton says, quite seriously mythologising the chivalric hero but he does not idealise him. The stupidity is as clearly seen as the chivalry; Douglas is well aware of the childishness of his 'heroes' and when the wounded soldier says: 'It's most unfair, they've shot

my foot off', the note of petulance and the prep-school vocabulary are used deliberately to point to this childishness and
also to contrast with the rhetorical rise in the next stanza:

> How can I live among this gentle
> obsolescent breed of heroes, and not weep?
> Unicorns, almost,
> for they are falling into two legends
> in which their stupidity and chivalry
> are celebrated. Each, fool and hero, will be an
> > immortal.

Perhaps more reticent in tone is the poem, *Gallantry*, but
there is no tightlipped insensitivity to be found in it. This
poem is closer in spirit to Sassoon and Owen than most of
Douglas's war poetry and the final stanza is strongly reminiscent
of Wilfred Owen's *The Last Laugh*:

> But the bullets cried with laughter,
> the shells were overcome with mirth,
> plunging their heads in steel and earth—
> (the air commented in a whisper).

I think it is fairly plain that he had read Owen and Sassoon but
their influence is only superficial. Douglas was far more
introspective than either of the Great War poets: there is something curiously private about his experience of battle and it is
a measure of his honesty that he does not pretend to feel more
pity for war's victims than in fact he does feel. 'The plains were
their cricket pitch / and in the mountains the tremendous drop
fences / brought down some of the runners' he writes in
Aristocrats: for him, the plains—that is, the battlefields of the
Western Desert—were the testing ground for his courage,
resolution, manhood. He does not, as both Sassoon and Owen
did, question the moral implications of fighting a war, of
killing his fellow men. He accepts what seems to be the

historical necessity as he accepts the ethic of his group and it was perhaps easier for him to do this since he was serving in the Tanks, fighting a kind of war which was very different from the one fought by the infantry, a war where the enemy was visible and to be met on more or less equal terms, one where individual decision and initiative were constantly being exercised.

Ian Hamilton writes: 'There is very little in Douglas, though, of the sheer documentary impact of reluctant recruits like Fuller and Lewis', and we know what he means by this. There is nothing in Douglas's poetry of the bleak wartime Britain of rationing, blackouts, austerity, boredom; nothing of the personal struggle against being absorbed and reshaped to a mindless pattern by the military machine, nothing of the desperate longing for private and domestic certainties that seemed lost forever. But Douglas was younger than either Roy Fuller or Alun Lewis, he was unmarried and, most important, he was involved in a shooting war as neither of the other two poets was. In fact there is considerable documentary observation in the Middle East poems, in the descriptions of the cities and of the desert. In *Landscape with Figures* he presents a bird's eye, or pilot's eye, view of the battlefield:

> Perched on a great fall of air
> a pilot or angel looking down
> on some eccentric chart, the plain
> dotted with the useless furniture
> discerns crouching on the sand vehicles
> squashed dead or still entire, stunned
> like beetles: scattered wingcases and
> legs, heads, show when the haze settles.

Later in the same poem he describes the dead bodies in terms similar to those used in parts of *Alamein to Zem Zem*.

> On scrub and sand the dead men wriggle
> in their dowdy clothes. They are mimes

who express silence and futile aims
enacting this prone and motionless struggle
at a queer angle to the scenery
crawling on the boards of the stage like walls,
deaf to the one who opens his mouth and calls
silently. The decor is terrible tracery
of iron. The eye and mouth of each figure
bear the cosmetic blood and hectic
colours death has the only list of.

The imagery here may strike some readers as too theatrical, but Douglas is not over-dramatising the scene. He is re-creating, not only the thing as it was, but the sense of unreality that the soldier in the desert experienced amidst such carnage and desolation, the protective film that came between the watching eye and the things observed.

The third and final section of the poem is less successful and could justifiably be called melodramatic; the intrusive first-person singular does seem to be striking attitudes in a windily rhetorical manner and for once a note of both self-pity and self aggrandizement creeps in. But this is rare in Keith Douglas's work and I believe that the best of his war poetry, with its hardness of edge, wit, vision, compassion and disciplined intelligence will prove to possess at least the lasting qualities of the best of Wilfred Owen.

Alun Lewis

Alun Lewis was just about as different from Keith Douglas in temperament, beliefs and in poetic aims and achievement as he possibly could be. He was of working-class origin, originally pacifist—though this attitude was reluctantly abandoned in the face of the inescapable facts of Hitler's military and political intentions—earnest and industrious, no admirer of the dandy or aristocrat, a man with strong moral and political convictions. From the testimony of his friends and the evidence of his letters it is clear that he was a good man, a devoted and loving husband, a person of stern integrity. There are in his letters[15] moments of gaiety and even, in the intimate ones to his wife, Gweno, passages of whimsy, but the gaiety is somehow a serious performance; one does not feel that it is spontaneous; it is self-conscious and decidedly literary:

> 'This is my love to you first and foremost, and from twenty singing birds in a cherry-ripe pie of kisses whipped in the white of egg. How's school? And the weather? And Venus? And Bombo? And you? Be you through thick and thin. I'm trying so hard to be me. And I will be.'

It is sometimes difficult to escape the feeling that Lewis was just a bit priggish and, despite his jolly spells, he lacked humour. In a letter to his friend, Richard Mills, dated November 1941, he wrote:[16]

'He (Robert Graves) warned me against becoming too democratic—poets are not democratic in their poetry but only in their lives. Do you accept? I don't. I wrote back and said that my whole power, such as it is, springs from one source—humility—which alone engenders and resolves my perpetual struggle against the arrogant and the submissive, the victors, and the vanquished. I think I am working from the only true source these days: if I succeed (I use the word in no vulgar sense) I will have helped to make the world gentler, more understanding, more beautiful therefore. I don't mind sweating my soul out for such an end.'

To boast so earnestly of his own humility shows a quite startling absence of a sense of the absurd and, while one can be touched by Lewis's *naïveté* and even salute it as an index to his honesty, doubts as to whether such opaque solemnity is desirable in a young poet cannot be stifled.

Lewis was born on July 1, 1915, at Aberdare and was educated at Cowbridge Grammar School, leaving in 1932 for the University College of Wales, Aberystwyth, where he took a first in History. From there he went to Manchester University to do post-graduate work in medieval history, returning with an M.A. to Aberystwyth in 1937. The following year, after qualifying as a teacher, he took a temporary post at a secondary school in Pengam in his native Glamorgan. As a teacher he seems to have been fairly successful and certainly he was popular with his pupils, but it is unlikely that he would have devoted himself seriously to the profession had he survived the war. He did not teach for long. In the spring of 1940, shortly before he was due to be conscripted, he volunteered for The Royal Engineers and was posted to Longmoor in Hampshire where *All Day It Has Rained* was written.

He was soon sick of the senseless mechanical duties he was called on to perform and he applied for a transfer to the Education Corps, a request which was finally turned down in January 1941. He then put in for a commission in the infantry, was accepted and posted to an OCTU at Morecambe from which he emerged as a Second Lieutenant under orders to join the South Wales Borderers at Woodbridge in Suffolk. Meanwhile he had married Gweno with whom he was deeply and—because of the

long separations and multiple uncertainties imposed by service
life—painfully in love.

He was not at ease as an infantry officer. With his background
of radical nonconformism (his grandfather was an agricultural
labourer who had been lured into the pits by what had seemed
the prospects of better money), his sense of justice, his hatred of
the sham, he could not accept without qualms the privileges
enjoyed by officers and he quickly came to see that he could do
nothing to redress the scandalous inequalities that existed
between officers and other-ranks. In the summer of 1942
Lewis's regiment was converted to tanks and the following year
he was posted to India.

He found the Far East both exciting and dismaying and he was
at first shocked by the passivity of the poor, but the stimulus of
new surroundings, a different world, supplied him with both
creative vitality and subject-matter for poems and short stories.
He was also naturally concerned with the imminent experience
of battle and the possibility of death and, like all soldiers on the
edge of combat, he could not be certain of how he would
behave under pressure.

In February 1944, Lewis's unit moved into Arakan to face the
Japanese but in fact he did not see military action in the full
sense at all. On March 5th, he died in circumstances that are
still by no means clear. Certainly he was not killed in battle. The
official history of his regiment describes his death as follows:[17]

> 'Although they heard shots about five hundred yards away on
> the first night, and were bombed by Japanese aircraft the next
> day, there was no contact with enemy ground forces, and the
> only Japanese they saw were prisoners being escorted back.
> At Goppe Pass the Battalion lost one of its most popular
> officers, their first Burma casualty. Lieutenant Alun Lewis, the
> Intelligence Officer, was accidentally wounded by a pistol
> shot; he died in the Casualty Clearing Station at Bawli and
> was buried in the little military cemetery alongside the river
> near Bawli Bridge.'

'Accidentally wounded by a pistol shot' is remarkably vague and
it is not surprising that rumour and speculation about what
really happened in Burma were active for a long time after his

death. There was even talk of politically motivated murder and, almost inevitably, suicide was suggested, but neither theory was supported by the least scrap of evidence. His death was tragic but precisely how it came about is not important. What is important in the study of his poetry is to realise that he was not a soldier-poet in quite the same sense that Owen and Sassoon were in the First World War and Keith Douglas was in the Second World War. He did not directly experience the terror, exultation, weariness and despair of battle and hammer out records of what he had endured. He was a soldier-poet of a different kind: the reluctant, unhappy warrior, suffering boredom, exasperation, loneliness, exile, frustration and anxiety, the civilian in uniform, fighting not the enemy in arms but the debilitating longing for the lost peace, for comfort and love. He was in some ways the representative poet of the Second World War.

Raiders' Dawn, Alun Lewis's first book of poems, was published in March 1942. It is an uneven collection and the weaker poems show very clearly the faults that are present, though less glaringly so, in some of his best work, a tendency to smother his substantives with thick adjectives, the use of clumsy and arbitrary alliteration and a verbal slackness, a lack of proper vigilance that permits some tired old poeticisms to infect the healthier parts of many of the poems, lines like 'I have left / The lovely bodies of the boy and girl / Deep in each other's placid arms . . .', 'The beautiful lanes of sleep . . .', 'My soul cries out with love . . .', and 'Beauty disfigured, / And the coward cruel brute / Shaping us in his image.'

Ian Hamilton writes in his essay, *The Forties*,[18]

'Alun Lewis . . . seems to me the most cruelly under-valued poet of the forties and it is interesting to see how a cliché-estimate of him has descended from guide to guide so that it is now, apparently, established as solid ground for ignoring him. The estimate says that Lewis was not really a poet, but a prose writer who had temporarily strayed into verse. It seems to have been originally based on an isolated remark of Lewis's and it first appears in the Penguin *New*

Writing obituary notice by Jack Marlowe, where it receives minimal critical support. Since then it has gone into general currency and no longer needs support; one finds it repeated by Stephen Spender in *Since 1939*, Kenneth Allott in his Penguin *Contemporary Verse,* and Anthony Thwaite in *Contemporary English Poetry*, in almost identical language and with an absolute identity of bald conviction.'

But perhaps the view of Alun Lewis as a natural prose writer rather than a poet is less of a 'cliché-estimate' than Ian Hamilton supposes for it seems to me obvious that Lewis would not allow the same kind of reach-me-down phrasing that disfigures much of his poetry to appear in his prose which is written with more care than a great deal of his verse. The carelessness to be found in much of his poetry might be almost deliberate, a consequence of a romantic attitude to the nature and function of the poet, a blurred notion that authentic poetry is 'inspired' and that it should come 'as naturally as leaves to a tree'. His poems were written very quickly. In a letter to his parents he writes:[19]

'Altogether they make 52 poems—17 written in England, 6 at sea and the remaining 30 out here. I suppose that's pretty good for twelve months.'

In another letter, also to his mother and father, he speaks of the writing of his short stories with a self-critical note that is not to be found in any of his references to his own poetry:

'I've been working hard at the short stories: mainly some new ones I'm trying to write. My touch isn't at all sure: my thoughts wander instead of crystallizing and I can't imagine the people objectively enough. So I've had to scrap several versions. I've written one three times, another twice, and I'm still dissatisfied. It's good practice, even though it's rather disheartening when I've got so little time for writing at all.'

In fact I would suggest that Lewis's poetry is often at its best when it is displaying virtues usually associated with good prose: I would go farther and say that his approach to the raw material of experience was often the way of the prose writer, and many of

his formal lyrics with their conventional ecstatics and invoca-
tions of 'barefoot lovers', 'golden hair', 'roses', 'the smiling
moon', and suchlike properties are little more than thin exer-
cises whose poeticisms hope to disguise the essentially prosaic
cast of the mind which has produced them.

The crucial difference between the poetic and the prosaic
uses of language has less to do with such matters as metre,
diction and imagery than with a special kind of verbal strategy
and aim. The prose use has as its goal the articulation and
embodiment of a concept which pre-exists in more or less
coherent shape in the author's mind before pen has been put to
paper. The prose writer's success or failure is to be judged by the
degree of approximation of the written composition to the
unwritten idea which he has attempted to clothe in language.
The poet, on the other hand, uses language as an instrument of
exploration: he judges the success or failure of his poem, not by
the extent to which it resembles the perfect platonic poem he has
been striving to emulate, for no such thing existed, but—formal
and textural elements aside—by the discoveries it makes, the
revelations about himself in relation to the experience he has
been investigating. There is always a sense of both discovery and
mystery about a true poem.

There is one very good lyric in *Raiders' Dawn* which is
uncharacteristically restrained and free from the lush and ready-
made images of many of the *Songs* and *Love Poems*. This appears
in the section *Poems in Khaki,* and is called *Christmas Holiday*:

Big-uddered piebald cattle low
The shivering chestnut stallion dozes
The fat wife sighs in her chair
Her lap is filled with paper roses
The poacher sleeps in the goose-girl's arms
Incurious after so much eating
All human beings are replete.

But the cock upon the dunghill feels
God's needle quiver in his brain
And thrice he crows: and at the sound
The sober and the tipsy men

Jump out of bed with one accord
And start the war again.

The fat wife comfortably sleeping
Sighs and licks her lips and smiles

But the goose-girl is weeping.

But it was not in his rather rare moments of lyric felicity that
Alun Lewis was representative of the common soldier who
served in the Second World War; it was because in some of his
most successful poems he speaks for the unhappy civilian who
had been pressed into service, and no one has written more
directly and accurately of the boredom and discomfort, the
slow, remorseless strangling of individuality, the crushing of the
spirit and imagination that almost every wartime soldier in the
ranks had to endure. *All Day it has Rained* is a pungent physical
evocation of military life under canvas in wartime England and
it also communicates the deadening indifference, the lassitude,
frustration and resignation that the khaki regime forced upon
even the most vital and sensitive spirits, a stupor that might
have been merciful had it been absolute but one which was
pierced by the continuous ache of yearning for the lost consolations of the civilian world.

And we stretched out, unbuttoning our braces,
Smoking a Woodbine, darning dirty socks,
Reading the Sunday papers—I saw a fox
And mentioned it in the note I scribbled
                                    home;—
And we talked of girls, and dropping bombs
                                    on Rome,
And thought of the quiet dead and the loud
                                    celebrities
Exhorting us to slaughter, and the herded
                                    refugees;
—Yet thought softly, morosely of them, and
                                    as indifferently

As of ourselves or those whom we
For years have loved, and will again
Tomorrow maybe love; but now it is the rain
Possesses us entirely, the twilight and the rain.

The poem ends with a reference to Edward Thomas, that fine
poet who was killed in the First World War in 1917, who:

> . . . . brooded long
> On death and beauty—till a bullet stopped his
> song.

Here, a note enters the poem to weaken it, a softness that
Lewis often found hard to resist. It is true that Edward Thomas
in his poetry did brood on death and beauty as did, of course,
almost every English poet of consequence, but he did not do so
in the way that Lewis's rather limp and euphemistic lines
suggest.

Edward Thomas was an important influence on Lewis and,
on the whole, a salutary one; in fact one of the best poems in
Raiders' Dawn is the one entitled *To Edward Thomas*. It is a
moving tribute to a poet Lewis admired and loved, and Section
III contains a descriptive passage in the rhythms and idiom of
the older poet, lines which, I am sure, Thomas would not have
been ashamed to own.

I sat and watched the dusky berried ridge
Of yew-trees, deepened by oblique dark shafts,
Throw back the flame of red and gold and
russet
That leapt from beech and ash to birch and
chestnut
Along the downward arc of the hill's shoulder,
And sunlight with discerning fingers
Softly explore the distant wooded acres,
Touching the farmsteads one by one with
lightness

> Until it reached the Downs, whose soft green
> > pastures
> Went slanting sea- and skywards to the limits
> Where sight surrenders and the mind alone
> Can find the sheeps' tracks and the grazing.
>
> And for that moment Life appeared
> As gentle as the view I gazed upon.

I find the ending, too, much more effective than the last lines of *All Day it has Rained*; it seems more deeply felt and thought and is expressed with more intensity and originality:

> . . . . I knew the voice that called you
> Was soft and neutral as the sky
> Breathing on the grey horizon, stronger
> Than night's immediate grasp, the limbs of
> > mercy
> Oblivious as the blood; and growing clearer,
> More urgent as all else dissolved away,
> —Projected books, half-thoughts, the children's
> > birthdays,
> And wedding anniversaries as cold
> As dates in history—the dream
> Emerging from the fact that folds a dream,
> The endless rides of stormy-branched dark
> Whose fibres are a thread within the hand—
>
> Till suddenly, at Arras, you possessed that
> > hinted land.

There are one or two other good poems in *Raiders' Dawn* including *The Public Gardens* where Lewis shows how the man in uniform can utilise the anonymity that his condition has forced him to accept to observe the strangeness and variousness of the non-military life that continues around him and, although his sense of isolation, of being excluded from the civilian

world of women and children and domestic comforts is strong
and melancholy in the poem, a hopeful strain is there, too, for
sympathy and imagination have not entirely atrophied in the
soldier and there are moments when:

> . . . . forgetting my khaki, my crude trade,
> And the longing that has vexed and silenced
> me all the day,
> Now simply consider the quiet people,
> How their pattern emerges as the evening
> kindles
> Till the park is a maze of diagonal lines, ah far
> Too fine to catch the sun like the glittering
> webs
> The spiders have folded and flung from the
> fading privet.

Another poem, *After Dunkirk,* begins weakly with some of
Lewis's worst generalised, unfocused ruminations and inflated
rhetoric:

> I have been silent a lifetime
> As a stabbed man,
> And stolid, showing nothing
> As a refugee.
> But inwardly I have wept.
> The blood has flown inwardly into the spirit
> Through the gaping wound of the world.
> And only the little worm,
> The small white tapeworm of the soul,
> Lived on unknown within my blood.

The poem picks up only when Lewis fixes his attention on the
physical facts of army life:

> And next, the rough immediate life of camp
> And barracks where the phallic bugle rules

The regimented orchestra of love;
The subterfuges of democracy, the stench
Of breath in crowded tents, the grousing
                         queues,
And bawdy songs incessantly resung
And dull relaxing in the dirty bar;
The difficult tolerance of all that is
Mere rigid brute routine; the odd
Sardonic scorn of desolate self-pity,
The pathetic contempt of the lonely for the
                         crowd . . . .

I think much of this is perceptive writing but it does seem to me to illustrate his basically prosaic approach to his subject-matter: he is at his best in the last six or seven lines quoted when he is making plain statements about things he has observed; when he tries the more decorative, imagic stuff—the 'phallic bugle' and 'The regimented orchestra of love'—I find him both strained and vague.

I cannot agree with Ian Hamilton[20] who finds Lewis's second and last collection of poems, *Ha! Ha! Among The Trumpets*, 'devitalized and prosy' compared with *Raiders' Dawn*, and once Lewis gets away from the flatulent and sentimental stuff in *Part One: England* and comes to grips with the fresh experiences of leaving England and soldiering overseas in *Part Two: The Voyage* and *Part Three: India* he produces some of his finest work, poems which are less well known than the widely anthologised pieces from *Raiders' Dawn* but are individual and memorable and long overdue the recognition they deserve.

As in his first collection he speaks for the bored and dejected conscript in sodden tent or freezing Nisson Hut, the inglorious suffering of loneliness and enslavement to the military machine, so in his second book he conveys poignantly the feelings of the same soldier when he is posted to a distant land to fight and probably die, feelings more ambiguous because, along with the even more painful sense of loss and separation from the loved persons and things of the civilian world at home, the sexual deprivation and longing, there is an excitement, a fearful anticipation of the ordeal of battle, an involuntary recognition of the terrible glamour of the possibility of death in action. There is also the fascination of being for the first time in a country so utterly different from anything hitherto seen, a stimulus that the writer welcomes though the loving husband deplores its origin.

On Embarkation contains some solid description and, apart from a few lapses ('The white delightful limbs, the nest of peace' and 'elusive as a dream'), it is a grave and honest piece of writing and, especially in Section III, a moving realisation of what wartime farewells were like:

> In all the ways of going who can tell
> The real from the unjustified farewell?
> Women have sobbed when children left for
> > school
> Or husbands took the boat train to pursue
> Contracts more tenuous than the marriage vow.
> But now each railway station makes and breaks
> The certain hold and drifts us all apart.
> Some women know exactly what's implied.
> Ten years, they say behind their smiling eyes,
> Thinking of children, pensions, looks that fade,
> The slow forgetfulness that strips the mind
> Of its apparel and wears down the thread;
> Or maybe when he laughs and bends to make
> Her laugh with him she sees that he must die
> Because his eyes declare it plain as day.·
> And it is here, if anywhere, that words
> —Debased like money by the same diseases—
> Cast off the habitual clichés of fatigue . . . .

Far from finding the poems in *Ha! Ha! Among The Trumpets* 'devitalized' I see them as developing a strength and sinew of which there is not much sign in *Raiders' Dawn* and poems like *A Troopship in the Tropics* and *Port of Call: Brazil* maintain a steady contact with the situations they deal with and show a steadfast rejection of the temptation to over-exploit dramatic possibilities

at the expense of total veracity, a gritty honesty which reminds
me of the best of W. E. Henley's sequence of hospital poems.
The lyrical pieces, too, are far more skilfully managed, poems
like *Water Music* and *Shadows,* and in *Song (On seeing dead bodies
floating off the Cape)* Lewis achieves the fine synthesis of thought
and feeling that he was groping for but infrequently finding in
his first book:

> But oh! the drag and dullness of my Self;
> The turning seasons wither in my head;
> All this slowness, all this hard s,
> The nearness that is waitir . my bed,
> The gradual self-effacement of the dead.

The love poem, *Ways,* is also very effective, owing perhaps
something to Edward Thomas in its ambivalence and imagery,
but still an original and sensitive exploration of the way that love,
to the exile, can be a burden as well as a precious gift:

> Love being gravel in the wound
> When the silent lovers know
> Swaying in the misty rain
> The old oppression of the burden
> Growing in them as they go,
> Though trees are felled and grow again,
> Far and farther each from each.
> Longing hardens like a stone.
>
> Lovers go but hardly, all alone.

Alun Lewis's most durable and original poems are, to my
mind, the ones in which he treats the Indian landscape, especially its wilder reaches, as an external correspondence or emblem
of certain attitudes and states of consciousness that he, the
Western invader, discovers in himself. In the best of these the
physical details are sharply seen and the sense of place is strongly

communicated but the poems are more than realistic pictures of an exotic country. He is able without strain or sleight of hand to universalise his personal dilemmas, the problems of coming to terms with the lover and the soldier, of preserving the creative virtues of imaginative sympathy, pity and love of justice while preparing to kill men, problems which he shared with every man in uniform and which he, as a poet, felt he had to articulate and explore. As he said of his poems in a letter to his wife:[21]

'They're universal statements if they're anything'.

One of these poems, *The Mahratta Ghats*, opens with a description of a dry, unproductive land where the natives struggle bitterly for bare survival:

> The valleys crack and burn, the exhausted
> plains
> Sink their black teeth into the horny veins
> Straggling the hills' red thighs, the bleating
> goats
> —Dry bents and bitter thistles in their throats—
> Thread the loose rocks by immemorial tracks.
> Dark peasants drag the sun upon their backs.

Then follow four lines where the bleakness is displaced by a mocking splendour:

> High on the ghat the new turned soil is red,
> The sun has ground it to the finest red,
> It lies like gold within each horny hand.
> Siva has spilt his seed upon this land.

The reference to Siva, the third deity of the Hindu triad who possesses the power of reproduction and dissolution, is, of course, ironic since his bounty is so exiguous and his worshippers are his victims. He is one of the 'small gods . . .' who 'suck

the marrow from their bones'. The poem ends with the oppres-
sed beggar and the exiled foreign soldier being identified, both
victims of political or religious processes against which they
are helpless.

> Who is it climbs the summit of the road?
> Only the beggar bumming his dark load.
> Who was it cried to see the falling star?
> Only the landless soldier lost in war.
> And did a thousand years go by in vain?
> And does another thousand start again?

The anatomical metaphors in the opening lines are perhaps a
little commonplace but the poem as a whole works very well
and the landscape is used effectively to image the dry wastes of
the heart in both soldier and beggar.

In the same letter to his wife referred to above Lewis wrote:[22]

'. . . And although I'm more engrossed with the *single* poetic
theme of Life and Death, for there doesn't seem to be any
question more directly relevant than this one, of what
survives of all the beloved, I find myself quite unable to
express at once the passion of Love, the coldness of Death
(Death is cold), and the fire that beats against resignation,
"acceptance". Acceptance seems so spiritless, protest so
vain. In between the two I live.'

In *The Journey* he attempts, with a large measure of success,
to explore the double theme of Life (or Love) and Death. The
poem begins:

> We were the forerunners of an army,
> Going among strangers without sadness,
> Danger being as natural as strangeness.
> We had no other urge but to compel
> Tomorrow in the image of today,
> Which was motion and mileage and tinkering

When cylinders misfired and the gasket leaked.
Distance exhausted us each night;
I curled up in the darkness like a dog
And being a romantic stubbed my eyes
Upon the wheeling spokeshave of the stars.

Here is the situation of the wartime soldier serving in a foreign land, his welcoming of the anaesthetic of routine which protects him against the pain of feeling too much the unhappiness of the beloved at home and guilt at his own rôle as a killing engine. This is followed by an excellent description of the jungle as the journey progresses and then, in the final section, the awareness of Death is explicitly introduced, the fear that, at some level of consciousness, is omnipresent in every soldier on the threshold of action. The anodyne of the unvarying procedures of military service, the sameness of the days, have reduced the man to a state close to that of the lower animals where only fear of death can touch his emotions and imagination:

There was also the memory of Death
And the recurrent irritation of ourselves.
But the wind so wound its way about us,
Beyond this living and this loving,
This calculation and provision, this fearing,
That neither of us heard the quiet voice
                              calling us,
Remorse like rain softening and rotting the
                              ground,
We felt no sorrow in the singing bird,
Forgot the sadness we had left behind.
For how could we guess, oh Life, oh suffering
                         and patient Life,
With distance spun for ever in the mind,
We among the camels, the donkeys and the
                         waterfalls,
How could we ever guess,
Not knowing how you pined?

Writing to Robert Graves, who was helping with advice and criticism to see *Ha! Ha! Among The Trumpets* through the press, Lewis refers to a poem 'about the jungle':[23]

> 'I've felt a number of things deeply out here; perhaps the jungle has moved me more deeply than anything else, the green wilderness where one has nothing but one's sense of direction and there is no alarm because there is the Sun and there is one's shadow and there is time—but when I wrote a poem about the jungle I found it had become a criticism of the Western world which in a measure I understand, but of the jungle I had said nothing. That happens nowadays with most of me. And I will have to abandon the vast for the particular, the infinite for the finite, the heart for the eye.'

It appears from the comment '. . . but of the jungle I had said nothing' that Lewis felt that he had not succeeded in what he had set out to do, but the poem he refers to is obviously the one called *The Jungle* and it seems to me among the best, if not the very best of his works in verse, for he says a good deal about the jungle, re-creating its physical presence and, without strain, using that presence for his symbolic purposes which give depth and scope to the poem which might otherwise have been a mere evocation of time and place. *The Jungle*, too, is organised with skill and the shifts from present to past, from the jungle to the urban squalors of the West, from objective concern with the sickness of society to subjective preoccupation with the individual soul, the limits of the human will and the importance of coming to terms with one's own mortality, these are managed most adroitly.

When he says in his letter to Graves '. . . I will have to abandon the vast for the particular, the infinite for the finite, the heart for the eye', he obviously speaks with regret as if, as a poet, he is accepting a necessary limitation but what has really happened is that he has arrived without knowing it at the salutary conclusion that the poet's job is to concentrate on the particular, something fully understood by men like Pound who said, 'Go in fear of abstraction' and Yeats who knew that 'Man can embody truth but cannot know it'. What Lewis did not seem to understand, at least in the letter quoted, is that concentration on the particular does not entail an abandonment of the vast but is a way of bringing it into focus and fixing it through correspondences, whereas an attempt to deal directly with the huge and abstract must end in myopia and impotence. Luckily for him and us instinct led him in *The Jungle* to focus on particulars from which he never wanders far into generalisation. Generalisation and reflection do exist in this poem but they always proceed naturally from, and are tied firmly to, image and circumstance.

The poem opens with seven lines which economically but vividly set the jungle scene:

> In mole-blue indolence the sun
> Plays idly on the stagnant pool
> In whose grey bed black swollen leaf
> Holds Autumn rotting like an unfrocked
>   priest.
> The crocodile slides from the ochre sand
> And drives the great translucent fish
> Under the boughs across the running gravel.

Then comes the human intruder who does not belong there, the foreign soldier, finding in the jungle a reflection of his own condition, the inertia, the freedom, which paradoxically is a kind of enslavement, from responsibility, from choice, even from feeling the desire for the darkness, for nothingness. Throughout the poem Lewis writes in the first person plural but only because he feels that he is representative of all men in this situation.

> . . . . fidelities and doubts dissolve,
> The weighted world a bubble in each head,
> The warm pacts of the flesh betrayed
> By the nonchalance of a laugh,
> The green indifference of this sleep.

The second section opens with a shift in time and place and also a change in viewpoint which moves outward to the social ills it looks upon as the poem tracks back to the:

> . . . . mines and offices and dives,
> The sidestreets of anxiety and want,
> Huge cities known and distant as the stars,
> Wheeling beyond our destiny and hope.

This bleak vision of Western civilisation ends with:

> The patient queues, headlines and slogans flung
> Across a frightened continent, the town
> Sullen and out of work, the little home
> Semi-detached, suburban, transient
> As fever or the anger of the old,
> The best ones on some specious pretext gone.

Then we return to the present and the jungle and the self-absorbed subjectivity of the end of the first section, but now the jungle is seen to represent the hope of something more affirmative and valuable; human life as observed in the depressed mining areas and industrial cities of Britain seems irremediably base or debased, political action futile, and the jungle appears to offer an alternative in the instinctual, unreflective life of nature, a prelapsarian world of beauty and innocence.

> But we who dream beside this jungle pool
> Prefer the instinctive rightness of the poised
> Pied kingfisher deep darting for a fish
> To all the banal rectitude of states,
> The dew-bright diamonds on a viper's back
> To the slow poison of a meaning lost
> And the vituperations of the just.

A key-word in this sentence is 'dream'. The poet knows that there is really no way back to such a world, and in the third section of the poem he probes deeply into the past and into his own heart, realising that:

> . . . though the state has enemies we know
> The greater enmity within ourselves.

But generalisation has not taken the poem over. The section begins with a striking image of the branches of the banyan trees obliterating most of the sunlight yet affording a kind of skylight through which memory and imagination can escape and voyage into the past:

> The banyan's branching clerestories close
> The noon's harsh splendour to a head of light.
> The black spot in the focus grows and grows:
> The vagueness of the child, the lover's deep
> And inarticulate bewilderment,
> The willingness to please that made a wound,
> The kneeling darkness and the hungry prayer;
> Cargoes of anguish in the holds of joy,
> The smooth deceitful stranger in the heart,
> The tangled wrack of motives drifting down
> An oceanic tide of wrong.

The section ends with a marvellous passage where Lewis, after generalising about the healing power of 'elemental love', addresses his actual human love:

> Oh you who want us for ourselves,
> Whose love can start the snow-rush in the
>   woods
> And melt the glacier in the dark coulisse,
> Forgive this strange inconstancy of soul,

The face distorted in a jungle pool
That drowns its image in a mort of leaves.

The language in this poem is more exact and, at the same time, richer than is usual in Lewis. The word, 'coulisse', here is surprising but not awkward: the alliterative echoes from 'snow' and 'glacier' are subtle and pleasing, the sibilants give us the sound of the flowing of the melted ice, and, of course, there is a delicate suggestion of sexuality if one wishes to pick it up. 'Mort', too, is fine with its double meaning of a great number and of death.

The fourth and final section begins with the poet being, as it were, again absorbed into the jungle, identifying with the 'Grey monkeys . . . ignorant and wise', those last epithets expressing again the romantic view of nature as a lost Eden, and observing that 'The distant world is an obituary, / We do not hear the tappings of its dread.' But later returns 'The old temptation to remould the world'. The human dilemma is inescapable. One cannot by an exercise of will become other than human, become 'ignorant and wise' like the jungle animals. The man who would become an animal becomes only a brutish man. The capacity for love is the greatest human virtue and it cannot be employed selfishly. It proceeds from sympathy, imagination and tenderness and these are the passions that force us to care, not only for a selected few, but for mankind.

The poem ends with a meditation on death, and here the reality of the jungle and the poet's consciousness are nicely fused:

The bamboos creak like an uneasy house;
The night is shrill with crickets, cold with
                                                          space.
And if the mute pads on the sand should lift
Annihilating paws and strike us down
Then would some unimportant death resound
With the imprisoned music of the soul?
And we become the world we could not
                                                          change?

Or does the will's long struggle end
With the last kindness of a foe or friend?

Poetry of this order and of the quality of many other Alun Lewis poems should not be undervalued because the author wrote a fair amount that was of a lower level of achievement. At his best Lewis has written work that deserves to stand with all but the greatest war poetry and no other writer of the Second World War has more truthfully and hauntingly recorded the sense of what it was like to endure the long monotony and dehumanisation of army life for the conscripted man in the ranks. The prevailing fashion for the gnomic and allusive or, at the other extreme, for disposable 'pop' verse, is sure to underrate a poet so serious, direct and explicit as Alun Lewis, but in doing so it demonstrates how unreliable it is as a guide to what is likely to give nourishment and lasting pleasure, to what is likely to endure.

Sidney Keyes

Both Keith Douglas and Alun Lewis, with all their differences
in style, purpose and achievement, can be seen as belonging to
that line of English poets, stretching from Chaucer to Hardy
and beyond, poets whose involvement with the bread and
meat of daily life, with the elemental experiences of birth,
growth, love, hate, joy and grief, fear and hope, was total;
whose subject-matter was always immediately at hand in the
experience, personal or vicarious, of the moment, and whose
myth-making was not the result of grandiose schemes to carve
great monuments in time but came naturally with their identi-
fication with the rest of humankind and the honesty and
vitality of their seeing and saying. Although both Douglas and
Lewis possessed good minds and were interested in the arts,
in ideas and in the life of the imagination, their first concern
was with the physical rather than the metaphysical, which
could look after itself, and they both strove to wrest their
message and music from the rhythms and idioms of the common
speech of their time and place and, however far they might have
travelled in space, each remained, as a poet, obdurately of this
island. The same cannot be said of the third young soldier-
poet who lost his life in the Second World War, Sidney Keyes.
  Keyes was not interested in reporting on his experiences as
a member of the fighting services during a global war, nor in
recording—except very occasionally and almost inadvertently—
his reactions to the prospect of facing combat. He was primarily

set upon producing literature, a poetry that would transcend the local and temporal circumstances in which it was created, and his principal influences or exemplars were the romantic and mystical poets, Rainer Maria Rilke and W. B. Yeats. The subject of war and his own involvement in it was treated mainly obliquely and the element of reportage, which had since 1914 come to be a feature of war poetry, was virtually absent. There were reasons, psychological and biographical, why this should be so.

Sidney Keyes was born on May 27, 1922, at Dartford in Kent, and his mother died only a few weeks after his birth. His father, an army officer, took only a casual and sporadic interest in him and Sidney was brought up by his grandparents. His grandfather, Sidney Kilworth Keyes, was a formidable character, physically powerful and autocratic, a successful miller who patented Daren flour, and a man whose rule over business and home was absolute. Young Sidney Keyes was a delicate child and considered not strong enough to attend school, so he was brought up for the first nine years of his life by a nurse. Fortunately for him he was highly intelligent and was able to master the art of reading at a very early age (he is said to have rejected, when he was only five, *The Children's Encyclopaedia* on grounds of inaccuracy) and, deprived of the companionship of other children, he created for himself a compensatory world of fantasy, drawing for its furnishings upon an imagination which had been nourished on the deeds of the heroes he had read about in history and legend. He was also fascinated by wild life and is said to have built up a small menagerie of birds, little animals and reptiles.

In 1931 Sidney's grandfather, who was over seventy years of age, married for the third time and his new wife was quick to decide that the boy should be sent to Dartford Grammar School where he stayed for three years before going on to Tonbridge, his father's old Public School. Here he was, it seems, quite happy though very reserved and, although he knew no Latin when he arrived, he reached the sixth form by the time he was sixteen and there he was lucky to have as his form-master, Tom Stavely, a poet as well as a sensitive and dedicated teacher, who instantly recognised the quality of Keyes's mind and verbal gifts and set about directing his reading and encouraging his original writing with tactful sympathy. It is not surprising that the schoolmaster was impressed by a boy of sixteen who could write a poem as accomplished and sophisticated as *Elegy* (*In memoriam S.K.K.*), which was written in memory of his grandfather:

> April again, and it is a year again
> Since you walked out and slammed the door
> Leaving us tangled in your words. Your brain
> Lives in the bank-book, and your eyes look up
> Laughing from the carpet on the floor:
> And we still drink from your silver cup.
>
> It is a year again since they poured
> The dumb ground into your mouth:
> And yet we know, by some recurring word
> Or look caught unawares, that you still drive
> Our thoughts like the smart cobs of your
> youth—
> When you and the world were alive.
>
> A year again, and we have fallen on bad times
> Since they gave you to the worms.
> I am ashamed to take delight in these rhymes
> Without grief; but you need no tears.
> We shall never forget nor escape you, nor
> make terms
> With your enemies, the swift departing years.

This is metrically inventive and assured and the conceits, especially 'the smart cobs of your youth', seem unforced and illuminating. I quote the poem in full because it does show that Keyes was perfectly capable of writing from a personal situation in a simple and direct manner, something which might seem doubtful to a reader acquainted only with his later attempts at vast universal utterances in a mode which reads like a cross between French symbolism and German expressionism.

In October 1940, he went up to Oxford as a History Scholar at The Queen's College and there he met and formed an enduring friendship with John Heath-Stubbs, who was a few years older than Keyes and a young man of considerable erudition and poetic skill. They had a lot in common: Heath-Stubbs had been almost blind from the age of sixteen and he had known a lonely and unhappy childhood during which he, too, had escaped into a self-created world of the imagination. He shared with Keyes a taste for ancient history and legend and it seems likely that his example and influence further encouraged the younger poet to turn away from immediate external reality to literature, mythology and the interior life for the sources of his poems. Most of the Oxford poems are not merely cloistered; they are claustrophobic and it would be virtually impossible to guess from a reading of them that they had been composed in wartime by a young man waiting to be called to the Colours.

During his first year at Oxford Keyes edited (with Michael Meyer) *Eight Oxford Poets* which included work by himself, Heath-Stubbs and Keith Douglas. In the rather scrappy and brief foreword to the anthology Keyes writes:[24]

'Our book is thus rather a group production than a representative anthology; most of the contributors having worked in very close touch with each other during the period. Nor is it altogether fanciful, we suggest, to trace certain elements common to the work of us all. We seem to share a horror at the world's predicament, together with the feeling that we cannot save ourselves without some kind of spiritual readjustment, though the nature of that readjustment may take widely differing forms. In technique, there is also some similarity between us; we are all . . . *Romantic* writers, though by that I mean little more than that our greatest fault is a tendency to floridity; and that we have, on the whole, little sympathy with the Audenian school of poets.'

Of that last remark one is tempted to say, 'So much the pity', for it is the young Auden qualities of wit, earthiness, and involvement with life as it is lived here and now, his irreverence and jokiness, an indispensable part of real seriousness, that would have helped Keyes away from the stifling mists of metaphysical romanticism towards a confrontation with the realities of immediate experience. There seemed a chance that the Army might dispel those mists but his reaction to the military life was to pull the blankets of quasi-mysticism and rhetoric over his head. In April 1942, the year that saw the publication of his first collection, *The Iron Laurel*, he was posted to Omagh in Northern Ireland, and in the following September he was commissioned in the Queen's Own Royal West Kent Regiment. In March 1943, he sailed for North Africa and on April 29th of that year he was killed in action after only a fortnight's experience of the Tunisian campaign. His Commanding Officer, Lieutenant-Colonel John M. Haycraft, gives this account of Keyes's tragically brief experience of battle:[25]

'Sidney Keyes came out with the Battalion to Algiers on March 10th, 1943; we moved up by sea to Bone, thence to the Beja sector where we took part in patrol skirmishes only; we then moved to Medjez area and did not, apart from the usual line-holding activity as before, have any serious actions until April 26th, when an attack was made in which Sidney did not take part. On April 29th, however, the battalion attacked a hill, Pt. 133, near Sidi Abdulla, in which Sidney's Company took part. His company, C, got its objective successfully during the night. His company commander, Braithwaite, sent Keyes forward with a patrol at dawn to find out the situation as regards the Boche in front. This patrol apparently ran into the enemy, who were forming up for a counter-attack on Hill 133. No survivor of this patrol has so far been found, and until I found Sidney's grave at Massicault I thought he was a prisoner.'

From the very beginning Keyes's verse showed a concern with death and pain that became almost obsessive, but it would be a mistake to infer from this that he was a masochist with a death-wish and that his early death was either foreseen or desired by him. In a letter to John Heath-Stubbs dated February 20, 1943, he wrote:[26]

'Please send me your death wish poem quickly, before the

general European death wish claims *me* (though under protest, and with the strongest desire for life, even to old age) . . .'

and in a letter to Renee-Jane Scott, written on the day before he was killed, appears this sad resolution:

'I shall have a lot more to say about this when the time for speaking returns. I cannot think that this campaign can last much longer; but after that, who knows! The only way back seems to be through armed Europe. I am not in much of a hurry, but I will get back *sometime* if it's humanly possible; and I've never yet failed to do anything I set myself to do. . . .'

There is no evidence of a longing for death there. No, it was the paraphernalia of romantic, literary death and pain that appealed to his youthful imagination so powerfully and as early as 1938 in his *Nocturne for Four Voices* he was writing Elizabethan and Jacobean pastiche rather similar to that of Thomas Lovell Beddoes, though naturally not so accomplished or macabre:

> My love's asleep all in the ground,
> The grass grows green on his grave-mound.
> He's lain there a year or more,
> Yet still I weep as I did before.
> His eyes were stars, his lips were coral-red:
> On his death-day we were wed.
> Death took my own, my sweetest boy—
> So come, sweet death, and be my joy.

Keyes said of this poem that it was '. . . an attempt at abstract (i.e. 'musical') poetry, a modification of the symphonic technique'. In other, less pretentious words, it is an example of of the work of a young man who is resolved to write poetry, even though he has nothing experiential to say and he is therefore obliged to borrow from the literature he admires and enjoys the themes and images he finds most dramatic and moving. Death is a popular subject with very young poets, but it is almost always the eloquent and theatrical death of the romantic play or poem which they find supplies them with a frisson which they hope will reverberate in their poetry. The props of greasepaint mortality and gothic romance are liberally scattered through Keyes's early poems: 'the moon's a swollen corpse', 'the clay—Our marriage bed', balustrades, balconies, graves, tombs, skulls and so on. It is interesting that his one early poem which is based on his observation of externals rather than on his reading or reflecting on subjective states of consciousness should be a description of Greenwich Observatory which takes absolutely no cognizance of the fact that a war, in which he must soon become an active participant, had been going on for over half a year:

> This onion-dome holds all intricacies
> Of intellect and star-struck wisdom; so
> Like Coleridge's head with multitudinous
> Passages riddled, full of strange instruments
> Unbalanced by a touch, this organism
> From wires and dials spins introverted life.
> It never looks, squat on its concrete shoulders,
> Down at the river's swarming life, nor sees
> Cranes' groping insect-like activity
> Nor slow procession of funnels past the
> > docks. . . .

The onion-dome of the Observatory might serve as paradigm for Keyes's own skull at this time, his own withdrawal from 'swarming life'; a glance at the titles alone of the poems he was writing during the period which saw the German conquest of Poland, the declaration of war by Britain and France, the German invasion of Denmark, Norway, the Netherlands and Belgium, the capitulation of France and the Dunkirk evacuation, the Battle of Britain and the entry of the U.S.A. and Russia into the war, shows just how cut off Keyes was from the outer world of action and event: *William Yeats in Limbo, Elegy for*

Mrs. Virginia Woolf, Paul Klee, Gilles de Retz, Plowman, St. John the Baptist, A Garland for John Clare, William Wordsworth, Troll Kings, Schiller Dying and so on.

In a footnote to his prefatory *Memoir* to *The Collected Poems* Michael Meyer writes:

'Keyes' literary and artistic preferences are curiously significant. For direction and inspiration, he turned to such visionaries as El Greco, Blake, Holderlin, Schiller, Rilke, Yeats and Sibelius. At the same time, he found his emotional problems most completely resolved in the writings of the nineteenth-century school of haunted countrymen: Wordsworth, Clare, Van Gogh, Hardy and, later, Housman and Edward Thomas. "I think I should have been born in the last century in Oxfordshire or Wiltshire, instead of near London between two wars," he wrote nine weeks before he was killed, "because then I might have been a good pastoral poet, instead of an uncomfortable metaphysical without roots. The trouble is, that a thing of beauty isn't a joy for ever to me; nor am I content to imagine that beauty is truth, etc. All I know is that everything in a vague sort of way means something else, and I want desperately to find out *what*."

He loved the masters of the macabre: Donne, Webster, Goya, Beddoes, Dickens, Picasso, Klee, Rouault, Graham Greene; and such as came his way of the early German and Russian films.'

A great deal has been made of Rilke's influence on Keyes's poetry, not least by Keyes himself, but I am not at all sure that it amounts to more than a sketchy borrowing of a few of Rilke's ideas to buttress his charnel images and give his vague romanticism some kind of intellectual respectability. Rilke—though to my mind a relentless bore—was a true visionary who genuinely believed that all phenomena were, in his words, 'equivalents' to some deeper metaphysical reality, and he saw everything that existed as a challenge to his powers of interpretation. 'Appearance and vision', he said, 'come together in the object.' But before the process of interpretation, that is to say the writing of the poetry could begin, the external phenomenon had to be observed, experienced, explored and assimilated before it could fuse with its metaphysical 'equivalent', and the trouble with Keyes was that his encounters with externality seemed to come almost entirely from reading or looking at paintings and scarcely ever from direct apprehension.

The most immediate literary influence on Keyes was W. B. Yeats and it can be seen in practically every poem he wrote before *The Foreign Gate* (March 1942)—this is well over half of his total output—and also in a good deal of the later work; in fact a number of his poems are not so much influenced by the great Irish poet as straight imitations of him.

William Yeats in Limbo is, of course, deliberate pastiche and clever enough for a boy of eighteen:

> Spirit-bodies loveliness
> Cannot expiate my pain:
> How should I learn wisdom
> Being old and profane?

But *A Renunciation* (October 1941) written nearly a year later is offered as Keyes's own voice and the accents of Yeats are just as strong:

> Strong angels bear God's canopy,
> Strong horseman ride the loose immoderate
>   wind;
> But O my dark girl from her balcony
> Laughs down and puts their glory out of mind.

And in the yet later *Images of Distress* (June 1942) one hears again the voice of the early Yeats:

> The wild gulls crying on the windy shore;
> The dark haired girl with summer in her face;

Silence the knocking stones inside my head,
Yet drive me out from every resting-place.

The first poem in which there is even a hint of Keyes being
aware that his country is at war is *Advice for a Journey* (March
1941) but his war is still a very 'literary' affair and waging it is
closer, it would seem, to mountain-climbing—or a romantic
poet's dream of climbing—than fighting in a platoon of
twentieth-century infantry:

> Never look back, not too far forward search
> For the white Everest of your desire;
> The screes roll underfoot and you will never
> > reach
> Those brittle peaks which only clouds may
> > walk.
>
> Others have come before you. The immortal
> Live like reflections and their frozen faces
> Will give you courage to ignore the subtle
> Sneer of the gentian and the iceworn pebble.
>
> The fifes cry death and the sharp winds call.
> Set your face to the rock; go on, go out
> Into the bad lands of battle, into the cloud-
> > wall
> Of the future, my friends, and leave your fear.

Even in the more mature and explicit *War Poet*, written just
before his enlistment, he seems to be writing less about the
year in which the Battle of El Alamein was fought than about
some time of legendary conflict:

> I am the man who looked for peace and found
> My own eyes barbed.
> I am the man who groped for words and found
> An arrow in my hand.

Of these lines Ian Hamilton remarks:[27]

'It seems typical of Keyes that it should be an arrow and not, say, a bren-gun. He finds it as impossible to treat of the materials, the concrete situations of modern warfare as he does to "sing" with what he calls "the foul tongue of a soldier"; it is usually "the soldier's drum", "the horse-hair plume" or, at best, "brass and iron".'

The comment is just, and when Keyes concludes his poem:

> When I grow sick or mad
> Mock me not nor chain me:
> When I reach for the wind
> Cast me not down:
> Though my face is a burnt book
> And a wasted town.

not only the 'chains' and the biblical-sounding 'cast me not down' but the syntactical inversions give one a strong sense of the archaic.

But it would be quite wrong to dismiss Keyes as a precocious author of pastiche. He possessed a fine ear and his skill at controlling a wide variety of verse-forms would have been admirable in any poet and is extraordinary in one so young. From the beginning he was a splendid phrase-maker:

> These balconies are empty, though the scent
> Of tender indecision wanders there;
> Let night proclaim their punishment
> Erasing gallant fictions from the air.
>
>   (*Lament for Dead Symbolists*)

> Frogs croak. The secret water,
> Muscular, fumbles blunt shoulders.
> No other sound. This glassy peace is spring.
>
>   (*Fragment: 'Shall the Dead Return?'*)

. . . Before the estuary lashed with pain, the
                                        sharp
Lift of the bar, and feel the tide making
                                    westward.
Then only in that drowned man's paradise
Of Hy Brasil or currentless Sargasso,
May the dead and the wind and the old woman
And her dog and my over-curious mind
Meet neighbourly and mingle without
                                    question.
                        (*The Anti-Symbolist*)

He was a stormy day, a granite peak
Spearing the sky; and look, about its base
Words flower like crocuses in the hanging
                                        woods,
Blank through the dalehead and the bony face.
                        (*William Wordsworth*)

and he wrote some really impressive dramatic monologues in a
flexible blank verse owing something, perhaps, to Eliot and
Browning, a form that was especially suited to his gifts, allowing
scope for his highly developed sense of the past and, through
its demand for historical verisimilitude, preventing him from
taking off too far into the misty spaces of metaphysical rumination. In short, it supplied him with subject-matter more clearly
defined and substantial than he usually tried to handle.

One of these monologues deals with a contemporary figure,
Marshal Timoshenko, the great Russian war-leader who was
born of peasant stock in Bessarabia. Keyes's imaginative
understanding goes deep of the cruel situation in which every
powerful general must find himself: the necessity to win the
campaign at whatever sacrifice of the lives of his own soldiers,
to make precedent love of country over love of his fellow men,
to accept the terrible loneliness of authority and command.

And there before the night, he was aware
Of the flayed fields of home, and black with
                                        ruin

The helpful earth under the tracks of tanks.
His bladed hand, in pity falling, mimicked
The crumpled hand lamenting the broken plow;
And the oracular metal lips in anger
Squared to the shape of the raped girl's
                     yelling mouth.
He heard the wind explaining nature's sorrow
And humming in the wire hair of the dead.

The soldier holds in his mind the torturing ambiguities and contradictions: 'the flayed fields of home' have been lashed mercilessly by war and 'fleeced' in the sense of 'impoverished'; the helpful earth is helpful in more ways than one: it has once helped those who cared for it to live; it may now offer shelter to the soldier taking cover as well as assisting the movement of the tanks. 'His bladed hand . . . mimicked the crumpled hand, etc.,', because his act copies the tired and resigned gesture of the peasant who must accept, though he cannot understand, the causes and effects of war, the peasant whom, except for the vagaries of providence, he himself might now be and, in a sense, still is. 'The oracular metal lips' are the mouth of invested power but they in their turn 'mimic' 'the raped girl's yelling mouth' (they are both victims of the same processes) and 'the wind . . . humming in the wire hair of the dead' is as much the sighing of his own grief and anger trying to communicate through the wire hair as it is the literal wind in the frozen hair of the corpses. The poem ends, a touch over-dramatically perhaps, but nonetheless movingly:

He turned, and his great shadow on the wall
Swayed like a tree. His eyes grew cold as lead.
Then, in a rage of love and grief and pity,
He made the pencilled map alive with war.

In arriving at an assessment of the value of Keyes's contribution to the poetry of the Second World War the fact must be taken into consideration that he was attempting something

quite different from any of his contemporaries. He may have
been misguided in his aims, though it is doubtful that he had
much choice when we consider the nature of his gifts, temperament and formative influences, but he pursued those aims
uncompromisingly. His conscious intention was to mytho-
logise his observations and experiences: '. . . to express the
eternal meaning which resides in the physical world, and show
the relationship between the eternal and its physical counterpart' and, when he wrote about war, he was resolved to distill,
as it were, the universal essence of the event by relating it
symbolically to previous wars and isolating the permanent
features from the temporal and ephemeral. He was, as he
himself stated, a romantic, but he had no truck with the
Apocalypse poets, that slightly farcical movement led by Henry
Treece, J. F. Hendry and G. S. Fraser, which encouraged a
kind of zany automatic writing, most of which read like a
drunken parody of Dylan Thomas.

In a letter to Richard Church in January 1943 Keyes wrote:[28]

'I don't even (consciously) follow the present trend towards
a new and over-wrought Romanticism. For these reasons I
find myself rather isolated as a writer; the poets I feel
kinship with are dead, yet many people who follow *them*
find me "advanced" and "obscure". The only living writers
whom I can accept entirely are Eliot, Charles Williams,
Graves (to some extent), my great friend John Heath-
Stubbs . . . and a few others—very few. As to the question of
my symbolism: the best clue that I can give you is to say
that I believe the greatest and most influential poets in the
last 100 years or so to be Yeats and Rilke. These two brought
back reports from a kind of Ultima Thule of Romanticism,
which suggest that there is even more—much more—to be
discovered there; and the starting point of my quest is
therefore an attempt to synthesize this information. When
I have fused and assimilated (if ever) this information, I shall
be ready to set out. The *Second Coming* and *Foreign Gate* are
my nearest misses so far. . . .'

The Foreign Gate was his first major attempt at realising his
ambition and, while as a whole it must be accounted a failure,

it is an interesting one with a number of incidental felicities. The poem takes as its epigraph these lines from Rilke's *Sixth Duino Elegy*:

> Wunderlich nah ist der Held doch den
> jugendlich Toten.
> . . . Das plötzlich begeisterte Schicksal
> Singt ihn hinein in den Sturm seiner
> aufrauschenden Welt.

In this work Keyes sets out to celebrate the heroic dead who, after their departure from the finite world, have become part of a timeless myth. We are told in a note that: 'Keyes began writing this at great pressure after he had already prepared the rest of *The Iron Laurel* for publication', and it carries many of the marks of over-hasty writing.

The Foreign Gate begins:

> Pillars of mist
> Mark the gate,
> Give passage to the mortal truant; guns
> Salute the end of gold- or moon-led fighter;
> Shrill shells and projectiles
> Divide the prison air and call the discontented
> Soldier from dreams of artificial hate.

The 'mortal truant' is the dead soldier or airman who has escaped from life and is welcomed at the 'Foreign Gate' which is a cemetery and at the same time an entrance to a kind of pantheon of warrior-heroes and lovers.

> The brother plucked out of a foreign sky
> To lie in fields of wreckage and white
> marble—
> He will remember easy speech again.

> The long-houred day
> Of freedom will return, and those who lie
> Out in the starshine comfortless
> Will find some small redress
> In speaking clear where the vague spirits
>   warble
> From their white foliage of bone . . .

I find '. . . vague spirits warble / From their white foliage of bone' imprecise and rather absurd. 'White foliage', literally 'leafage', is not a happy metaphor to describe 'bone' and 'warble', for me, echoes its comic morphemes, 'burble' and 'gargle'. I am not at all sure what Keyes is getting at here and, rightly or wrongly, I suspect that he is not too sure either, but I take it that he is equating the deed of physical heroism with poetry: one is the noble, sub-vocal speech of action, the other the heroic use of language.

Section II seems obscurely to continue this idea and it ends with a Rilkean exhortation:

> I am the fabled and symbolic tower
> People with eagles, and the deadly
> Bird-calling lighthouse in a storm of war.
> I am the columbarium of winged
> Souls, full of wind and windblown prayer.
> O see, poor crazy frozen flyers
> My refuge for you; travellers
> Lost in confusion by a foreign gate,
> My bridge for you; and voiceless speakers,
> Cry through the trumpet of my fear and rage.

That 'full of wind and . . .' is another unfortunate carelessness which suggests over-hurried composition and little revision.

The third section shifts from martial hero to the lovers from legend and history and the eternal oppositions of Summer and Winter (personified in the figure of Adonis who was restored to life by Proserpine on the condition that he spent

half the year with her and the other half with Aphrodite), fire
and ice, light and darkness, life and death, the unalterable
dualities which are interdependent yet irreconcilable and image
the condition of sexual love between man and woman. This
part of the poem closes with some fine romantic stuff:

>   . . . . Then the separation
>   That cannot be complete;
>   The calling spirits that may never meet;
>   The shattered engine sabotaged by time;
>   The locked cogs sundered each from each—
>   Imperfect to the Greek or shaped
>   Subtly by Satan to the prudish Mani.
>   Whichever way, eternity is crying
>   Out of the cold, out of the fiery wood—
>   And never separate;
>   Bound in unlucky fate
>   To riven mind and tumult in the blood.
>
>   They wander through my sleep and shame my
>   speaking:
>   The green star weeps and glimmers through
>   the wind.
>   There is no separation, but no meeting
>   Between the fire and ice.
>
>   The probing mind
>   Of poet cannot reach to comfort them;
>   Between the deadly trees they call and pace.
>   The young god never hears
>   And astral tears
>   Splinter like diamonds on his ravaged face.

   Section Four starts with a solemn funeral march for the dead
of many wars, ancient and more recent, including a reference
to Dunkirk, and it attempts to create a continuum where the
present suffering, waste and desolation of the Second World
War is seen as a part of a vast and timeless process:

'At Dunkirk I
Rolled in the shallows, and the living trod
Across me for a bridge . . .'
                'Let me speak out
Against this sham of policy, for pain
Alone is true. I was a general
Who fought the cunning Africans, returned
Crowned with harsh laurel, frantically cheered
Through Roman streets. I spoke of fame and
                                        glory.
Women grabbed at my robe. Great poets
                                praised me.
I died of cancer, screaming, in a year.'
'I fell on a black Spanish hillside
Under the thorn-hedge, fighting for a dream
That troubled me in Paris; vomited
My faith and courage out among the stones. . . .'
'I was a barb of light, a burning cross
Of wood and canvas, falling through the
                                        night.'
'I was shot down at morning, in a yard.'

The fifth part of *The Foreign Gate* makes its explicit ac-
knowledgement to Rilke:

Once a man cried and the great Orders heard
                                        him:
Pacing upon a windy wall at night
A pale unlearned poet out of Europe's
Erratic heart cried and was filled with speech.
Were I to cry, who in that proud hierarchy
Of the illustrious would pity me?
What should I cry, how should I learn their
                                        language?
The cold wind takes my words.

And the poem continues to re-state in over-rich language and imagery the idea of warrior-hero, lover and poet as having conquered death by:

> . . . . embracing bravely the white limbs,
> Engulfed in the long shining hair, they learnt
> Humility and triumph.

The poem ends with a more disciplined section that, in parts, owes much to T. S. Eliot:

> The great have come and the troubled spirits
>   have spoken:
> But hope or help is none till the circle be
>   broken
> Of wishing death and living time's
>   compulsion,
> Of wishing love and living love's destruction.
> Till then, the soul is caged in brain and bone
> And the observant man must walk alone.
>
> Mirrors and white perspectives of despair
> Surround the seeker:
> Words pass like figures in a windblown fire;
> The gabblings of unsatisfied desire
> Confound the speaker.
> The country of unfinished monuments
> Troubles my vision:
> It is well to remember the stone faces
> Among these ruins.

Eliot, too, is the principal influence behind Keyes's last ambitious poem, *The Wilderness*, which is again filled with images and symbols, the meanings of which one cannot often be sure. The 'wilderness' of the title is the desert into which Christ, Saint Anthony and numerous other holy men have retreated to purge themselves of pride and sensuality:

Here where the horned skulls mark the limit
Of instinct and intransigent desire
I beat against the rough-tongued wind
Towards the heart of fire.

The wilderness is also, one feels, something much more
personal, the hard excoriating experience of love, not erotic
love only, though including this, but all kinds of human love:

I say, Love is a wilderness and these bones
Proclaim no failure, but the death of youth.
We say, You must be ready for the desert
Even among the orchards starred with
blossom,
Even in spring, or at the waking moment
When the man turns to the woman, and both
are afraid.
All who would save their life must find the
desert—
The lover, the poet, the girl who dreams of
Christ,
And the swift runner, crowned with another
laurel:
They all must face the sun, the red rock
desert,
And see the burning of the metal bird.
Until you have crossed that desert and faced
that fire
Love is an evil, a shaking of the hand,
A sick pain draining courage from the heart.

I do not find that *The Wilderness* is any more of a success than
The Foreign Gate. Both poems reach to some region beyond
their author's grasp, they are both confused and, in parts, a
little absurd. Yet it must be remembered that they were both
written under difficult circumstances by a boy of twenty and,
with all their failings, they are undeniably impressive and, at

times, moving and memorable. It would also be idle to regret his veneration for and attempts to emulate Rilke, though it does seem to me that his best poems are the most direct where he allows his lyric gift free rein, poems like *A Garland for John Clare, Lover's Complaint, Lament for Harpsichord: the Flowering Orchards, To Keep Off Fears* and *The True Heart:*

> Those who land here, the restless and the
> lonely,
> Lay down their fears at last in shifting graves:
> The crippled spirit hides its long infirmity
> Among the tangle of these crystal waves.
>
> Guarded from love and wreck and turbulence
> The sad explorer finds security
> From all distraction but the thin lament
> Of broken shells remembering the sea.

It is believed that Sidney Keyes wrote some poems while he was on active service, but none of these has survived. Had he come through the war and experienced relationships of an earthy kind with men and women of flesh and blood and outgrown his infatuation with Rilke and cloudy symbolism he would almost certainly have developed into a poet of great importance. As it is, he certainly deserves to be remembered and to be read.

Roy Fuller

Neither Keith Douglas nor Sidney Keyes showed in their poetry any concern with social or political problems, indeed it would be impossible to say from a reading of their verse in what direction their political sympathies lay, and Alun Lewis, though in his private life firmly on the side of social egalitarianism and justice, wrote little poetry that could be called committed in the sense that it was written from a coherent ideological position towards which it hoped to draw the reader's sympathies. Roy Fuller, who served in the Royal Navy and happily survived the war to win high regard as poet, novelist and, until recently, Professor of Poetry at Oxford, was a different kind of writer; he was twenty-nine years old when he was called up and had been writing and publishing poetry during the thirties and had already forged for himself a style which, with little adaptation, would be able to deal with the experiences of service life in time of war. This style owed a good deal to the more solid elements in Auden's poetry: the accommodation of contemporary speech rhythms within prescribed verse-forms, imagery drawn from the familiar objects of twentieth-century urban life, the employment of unexpected but precise epithets, the ability to sustain argument without lapsing into prosiness and to modulate from the colloquial to the lyrical or restrained rhetorical without grinding the gears. If Fuller lacks some of the formal brilliance, versatility and occasional magic of Auden he also escapes the daftness, the arch chumminess that sometimes

95

deface Auden's poems. I do not mean to suggest that
Fuller's poetry is dull; on the contrary it is witty, intelligent
and almost invariably honestly and deeply felt, but sometimes
his approach to his material seems a little too tight-reined so
that while he has things in common with Auden and, to a lesser
extent, MacNeice, he is rather slower on his feet than the
first and carries a bit more weight than the second, lacking
something of the sparkle of both.

Fuller's political commitment at the outbreak of the Second
World War was unequivocal. He was a convinced Marxist and
he believed and hoped that one of the consequences of the war
would be a revolution which would result in a breakdown of the
class-structure in English society. He has written:[29]

'I had got to know something of working-class life in
left-wing politics during my early twenties: the first part of
my war service confirmed in a practical way the necessity for
social revolution, not least for the middle-class intellectual. It
extricated me from the great problem of the thirties—how to
live and write for a class to which one didn't belong. Such
extrication was mainly subjective, but there is certainly a
simplification and greater concreteness in the first poems I
wrote after calling-up, and I think the Marxist conception of
things underlies them in a less strained and dragged-in way
than hitherto.'

But this perhaps rather naïve belief in social revolution did not
survive for long, and one could say that much of Fuller's war
poetry is a record of disillusionment, not the disillusionment of
a Sassoon, whose dream of heroic adventure and ennobling
sacrifice was filthied and blood-soaked in the rat-infested
trenches of Flanders, but the bitter disappointment on witness-
ing a passionately held political ideal shattered by the realities
of an historical situation. In an early wartime poem, *Autumn
1940*, he writes of 'the sewers full of people', 'The bombers,
black insect eggs, on the sky's broad leaf' and images of the
presence of death during the London blitz proliferate, but he
manages to end on a note of political optimism with the very
thirtyish lines:

But where the many are there is no death,
Only a temporary expedient of sorrow
And destruction; today the caught-up breath—
The exhalation is promised for tomorrow.

And changed tomorrow is promised precisely
                                        by
The measure of the engendered hate, the hurt
Descended; the instinct and capacity
Of man for happiness, and that drowned art.

This was written before Fuller was conscripted into the Navy in April 1941 and, after a year or so of service as a rating, his poetry reflected different and more sombre attitudes to his experience of war. While he remained conscious of the wider social and political implications of the conflict, he saw no practical cure for the spreading infection of capitalist imperialism and the injustices fostered by a society whose values were incorrigibly materialistic and whose privileges and rewards were granted to wealth and rank, and his poetry became more pessimistic, more concerned, too, with his own situation as an individual and as a representative of his own kind, a middle-class Marxist intellectual, recently married, abruptly forced into a way of life that was calculated to stifle all within him that he most valued. One of the things that most appalled him was the reductive power of wartime service life, erotic love reduced to crudest lust, strength to aggression, wit to mechanical and obscene invective, leisure to boredom, justice to expediency, and the individual to a faceless number. In his *ABC of a Naval Trainee* he wittily lists in alphabetical order the miseries and the few small consolations of life as a naval rating, but the poem ends seriously enough:

S   is the silence for brooding on violence.
T   is the toughness imparted to all.
U   is the unit that never will clown it
Again as the lonely, the shy or the tall.

V   is the vastness: as actor and witness
We double our role and stammer at first.
W   is war to start off the quarries—
Our everyday hunger and every night thirst.

X   is the kiss or the unknown, the fissure
In   misery stretching far back to the ape.
Y   is the yearning for Eden returning:
Our ending, our Z and our only escape.

'The yearning for Eden', a natural reaction from a sensitive man to the corruptive forces all about him, the yearning for the relative happiness and innocence of the pre-war state, informs a lot of Fuller's war poetry, but he generally avoids the danger of being seduced into maudlin nostalgic reverie. Fuller saw little, if any, action during the war; after completing his basic training as an Ordinary Seaman he specialised as a radar mechanic and worked in East Africa on radar maintenance and reached the non-commissioned rank of Petty Officer. In November 1943 he returned to England, was commissioned and eventually found himself 'an officer, and a chair-borne one at that' at the Admiralty. During the war he came close, in a sense, to remaining a civilian but one who could pass freely among the closed society of the lower deck with a full understanding of the language used and the rites practised. In other words he maintained a reserve, a detachment, that permitted him to observe his fellow-matelots and their situation, which was, of course, his own situation, with unusual objectivity, but this objectivity by no means precluded passionate feeling.

In *Spring 1942*, which he wrote just before leaving England, he takes a simple incident of a naval chaplain coming up to a group of ratings who are lazing around, smoking, during a break from their duties, and the clergyman delivers a little homily, in the event rather an ill-judged one. He speaks of the great abstractions—'Freedom', he said, and 'Good' and 'Duty'— and, to the sailors, stunned by routine, boredom, the uniform drabness of existence and the menace of the future, the words are entirely without meaning—'We stared as though a savage spoke'—and one sees their blank gaze of utter non-comprehension. The poem ends with a cry of despair that contrasts very sharply with the facile conclusion of *October 1940*:

> And we made no reply to that
> Obscure, remote communication,
> But only looked out where the flat
> Meadow dissolved in vegetation.
>
> And thought: O sick, insatiable
> And constant lust; O death, our future;
> O revolution in the whole
> Of human use of man and nature!

One of the strands that went to forming the fabric of the serviceman's oppressive sense of dehumanisation, ennui and fear was 'the constant lust' Fuller speaks of here, though perhaps 'lust' is too vigorous a word for the sluggish randiness that seemed always present in the semi-monastic but sex-haunted atmosphere of barrack and training camp. Fuller captures this muffled, sadly unimaginative, brutal or sentimental sexuality very well in a number of poems; in fact he re-creates in his verse, more strongly than any other poet known to me, the physical sense of wartime England as experienced by con-scripted man. *Royal Naval Air Station* unfussily selects the details of barrack-room existence and sets them down with precision: the piano playing a sentimental tune, the rain at night, the pin-ups on the walls and the recognition that the trite lyrics of the popular songs did in fact contain a kind of truth and feeling, that they were the poetry of the inarticulate and scarcely literate:

> And the songs of the minute walk into our
>   ears;
> Behind the easy words are difficult tears:
> The pain which stabs is dragged out over
>   years.

Then the inconsolable sense of separation from the loved woman, the loneliness, intensified at night, the loss of identity and, behind it all, anxiety and the fear of death:

> A ghost has made uneasy every bed.
> *You are not you without me* and *The dead*
> *Only are pleased to be alone* it said.
>
> And hearing it silently the living cry
> To be again themselves, or sleeping try
> To dream it is impossible to die.

Fuller's more personal love poems are particularly effective. In these he does not make the conventional gestures of romantic love poetry but writes with a kind of bleak tenderness appropriate to the situation and with an honesty that is prepared to recognise the essential egoism of erotic love and the fact that fear is one of its strongest components.

> Love, the invaders of your mortal shape,
> The thought of those marauders, chill me so
> That now, as you lie helpless and asleep,
> Only my fear is real and ghostly go
> The bed, the chair, the clothes and all the rest
> Of this particular moment of our story—
> The slender guns, the nervous purple coast,
> The time of war which is the time of history.
>
> (From *Illness of Love*)

In *The End of a Leave* which describes a parting at night on a railway station the sense of both the fragility and strength of individual human love opposed to the annihilating powers let loose in the world is touchingly conveyed

> Suddenly our relation
> Is terrifyingly simple

> Against our wretched times,
> Like a hand which mimes
> Love in this anguished station
> Against a whole world's pull.

What is satisfying about the poems which have their roots in personal situations is the way in which they reach out from their private origins to find the general truths that the experiences point towards, truths which will strike chords of sympathetic recognition in all who have shared similar moments of separation, longing and the fear of loss.

Fuller's posting to East Africa seems to have provided a stimulus to his poetry, if only by supplying him with images derived from a fresh and exotic landscape, the spectacle of an alien, more primitive culture in the later stages of being changed or destroyed by western influences, and, at first, we find him at least partly turning away from the subjective themes of love and personal unhappiness to broader historical and political preoccupations. *The Green Hills* is a direct criticism of the corrupting influences of western capitalist values on a simple tribal society. It begins with some physical description of the landscape:

> The green, humped, wrinkled hills: with such
> > a look
> Of age (or youth) as to erect the hair.
> They crouch above the ports or on the plain,
> Beneath the matchless skies, are like a strange
> Girl's shoulders suddenly against your hands.

These lines show less precision than Fuller usually commands in his scene-setting. One can see what he is getting at in the first two lines. The texture of the hills appears to be wrinkled like the flesh of the very old or the newly born and their antiquity stirs feelings of awe, but the erecting of the hair seems to me both hyperbolic and slightly comic and there is not enough power in the foregoing images to justify the extremity of response.

'Matchless' is an uncharacteristically slack epithet and the 'girl's shoulders' image strikes me as over-contrived, but after this the poem improves, the observation becomes sharper as the contrast is shown between the surviving customs, the vitality and strangeness (The girls run up the slope, / Their oiled and shaven heads like caramels.) and the squalid intrusion Of '. . . corrugated / Iron, the wicked habit of the store.', the substitution of a more complex economy and the profit motive in place of simple barter. The criticism of western capitalist imperialism is made quite directly in the last stanza (the poem is written in three, each containing nine pentameters) and it demonstrates Fuller's ability to conduct an argument by correlating a logic of images with a logic of the mind:

> The poisoner proceeds by tiny doses,
> The victim weaker and weaker but
>   uncomplaining.
> Soon they will only dance for money, will
> Discover more and more things can be sold.
> What gods did you expect to find here, with
> What healing powers? What subtle ways of life?
> No, there is nothing but the forms and colours,
> And the emotion brought from a world already
> Dying of what starts to infect the hills.

The sickness is diagnosed but no prescription for a cure is written out. In his poem *The Giraffes* he uses the creatures as emblem of an order of existence that cannot be experienced by man, their total acceptance of what they are, their incuriosity, their apparent lack even of fear—'Those creatures walking without pain or love'—but the poem is inconclusive: we do not know whether the poet finds their indifference, their incapacity for feeling, enviable or not. At this stage it appears that Fuller, while unable to reaffirm his faith in Marxism as a panacea for the social sickness he sees on all sides, is also unable to abandon the creed completely since he would then be left without any guide in the gathering and engulfing darkness.

Plains continues his observing and brooding over the wild

animals he sees in the land of his exile and the conclusion
edges towards an equation of the animal and human which, if
totally accepted, would induce political despair.

> The next day, over all
> The sun was flooding and the sky rose tall.
> Where rock had weathered through the soil I
> saw
> A jackal running, barking, turning his head.
> Four vultures sat upon the rock and pecked,
> And when I neared them flew away on wings
> Like hair. They left a purple scrap of skin.
> Have I discovered all the plains can show?
> The animals gallop, spring, are beautiful,
> And at the end of every day is night.

The Tribes further charts the progress of his disillusionment as
it notes the cruel and repulsive practices of primitive cultures:

> I think of the tribes: the women prized for
> fatness
> Immovable, and by a sympathetic
> Magic sustaining the herds,
> On whose strange humps sit birds,
>
> And those with long dung-stiffened capes of
> hair,
> And those that ceremonially eat their dead;
> The ornamental gashes
> Festered and raised with ashes;
>
> The captured and dishonoured king compelled
> To straddle a vertical and sharpened stake,
> Until, his legs hauled at,
> The point bursts from his throat;

But when the attention switches to the ways in which the white

man has civilised the tribes 'Among the corrugated iron and /
The refuse bins where rats / Dispute with them for scraps'
Fuller discovers that progress has imposed on the Africans a
European sense of guilt and robbed their tabus of their power
to terrify, sustain and control:

> On waste plots and in the decrepit shanties
> They begin to discover the individual,
>   And, with the sense in time
>   Of Adam, perpetuate crime.
>
> The most horrible things you can imagine are
> Happening in the towns and the most
>   senseless:
>   There are no kings or poison,
>   Are laws but no more reason.

For Fuller, the poet, his experience of the war was both
valuable and terrible. As a socialist he held the Pelagian view
that man could attain perfection on earth, that evil was not the
consequence of the Fall but had social causes which could be
rectified through the exercise of reason and good will, but his
life among the working-class men, who were his companions in
the navy, and his awareness of all that was happening in the
world did little to buttress that view and his intellectual honesty
would not permit self-deception. In *Autumn 1942* he wrote:

> It is the news at which I hesitate,
> That glares authentically between the bars
> Of style and lies, and holds enough of fears
> And history, and is not too remote.
>
> And tells me that the age is thus: chokes back
> My private suffering, the ghosts of nature
> And of the mind: it says the human features
> Are mutilated, have a dreadful lack.

It half convinces me that some great faculty,
Like hands, has been eternally lost and all
Our virtues now are the high and horrible
Ones of a streaming wound which heals in evil.

This poem, and the moving meditation on time and action
called *Sadness, Theory, Glass,* in which '. . . The present is / A
lucid but distorting medium' are steps towards one of his
finest political war poems, *What is Terrible.* Here he speaks
directly and powerfully of what war means to him as a private
individual and as a representative of the human race. The poem
is written in five line stanzas with a regular pattern of rhymes or
near-rhymes and the language is continuously satisfying to both
ear and intellect. In making its large and explicit statement it takes
chances that not many poets of our time are prepared to take and
this willingness to risk banality or charges of egoism and
rhetorical posturing is a measure of Fuller's deep seriousness:

This apprehension has come slowly to me,
Like symptoms and bulletins of sickness. I
Must first be moved across two oceans, then
Bored, systematically and sickeningly,
In a place where war is news.

'In a place where war is news', that is to say a naval station
situated far away from where the fighting is going on but also
far away from home and all which that word meant to the
lonely and displaced exile trapped in a situation where boredom
became something quite different from the civilian's knowledge
of the feeling, something almost lethal in its debilitating relentlessness and was probably exacerbated by the guilt of the non-
combatant and certainly by the monotony of routine and the
lack of distractions. The poet recognises the wretchedness of his
situation—'fear, my misspent time, / My love, hurt and post-
poned . . .'—but he also recognises that the elemental oppositions
of war reduce in scale the conflicts of peace and, in many cases,
expose their triviality or falsity:

> Because in the clear hard light of war the
> ghosts
> Are seen to be suspended by wires, and in
> The old house the attic is empty: and the
> furious
> Inner existence of objects and even
> Ourselves is largely a myth: and for the sin
>
> To blame our fathers, to attribute vengeance
> To the pursuing chorus, and to live
> In a good and tenuous world of private values,
> Is simply to lie when only truth can give
> Continuation in time to bread and love.

The last two stanzas end on a note, not so much of hope as wistfulness: the 'if' in the conditional clause of the final sentence is coloured with doubt by all in the poem that has led to it:

> The year, the month, the day, the minute, at
> war
> Is terrible and my participation
> And that of the world is terrible.
> My living must now bear the laceration
> Of the herd, and always will. What's done
>
> To me is done to many. I can see
> No ghosts, but only the fearful actual
> Lives of my comrades. If the empty whitish
> Horror is ever to be flushed and real,
> It must be for them and changed by them all.

In the poems which succeed *What is Terrible* we find little sign of political hope and the growing sense of disillusionment at times approaches despair. In *Upon a Revolutionary Killed in the War* an explicit mistrust of all political action is expressed and elsewhere, as in *War Letters,* he turns to the theme of personal love and its special vulnerability to erosion in time of war and war's prolonged separations. Again, in the fine poem *Crusta-ceans,* he moves towards the view of mankind and its blind endeavours as being little different from the lower animals and, in *The Petty Officers' Mess* the despair of the intellectual and idealist when faced by the stunted aspirations of Everyman is voiced with a precise eloquence:

> The monkeys near the mess (where we all eat
> And dream) I saw tonight select with neat
> And brittle fingers dirty scraps, and fight,
> And then look pensive in the fading light,
> And after pick their feet.
>
> They are secured by straps about their slender
> Waists, and the straps to chains. Most sad and
> tender,
> They clasp each other and look round with
> eyes
> Like ours at what their strange captivities
> Invisibly engender.

The brutalising effects of service life in wartime appear again in *The Legions* in which the poet sees, without much hope, a return to peacetime existence:

> Then
> Shall we be free? And turn for home, as lean
> And baffled wolves turn for their starving den?
> Or shall we merely look upon our nails
> And see what kind of beasts we have
> become . . .

When a note of affirmation is sounded it is a muted one and it comes with the recognition that the view of mankind which sees human beings as units in a vast programme, the historical view, leads to no utopian solution of the problems of suffering but to a betrayal of the human which, despite the processes of brutalisation it undergoes, remains obstinately separate from the animal. In *The Statue* Fuller describes the statue of a horseman, a warrior—'Distilled from some sad, endless, sordid period of time'—seen in a harbour into which the poet's ship has sailed. Then he observes at night one of his comrades:

> Last night between the crowded, stifling decks
> > I watched a man,
> Smoking a big curved pipe, who contemplated
> > his great wan
> And dirty feet while minute after tedious
> > minute ran—
>
> This in the city now, whose floor is permanent
> > and still,
> Among the news of history and sense of an
> > obscure will,
> Is all the image I can summon up, my
> > thought's rank kill;
>
> As though there dominated this sea's
> > threshold and this night
> Not the raised hooves, the thick snake neck,
> > the profile, and the might,
> The wrought, eternal bronze, the dead
> > protagonist, the fight,
>
> But that unmoving, pale but living shape that
> > drops no tears,
> Ridiculous and haunting, which each epoch
> > reappears,
> And is what history is not. O love, O human
> > fears!

One of Fuller's most ambitious works of the Second World War is the sequence of nine linked sonnets called *Winter in Camp* which was written after his return from East Africa to England

and in these verses he attempts to clarify his attitudes towards many of the concerns which appear in his other poems, the relations between art and external reality, the inadequacy of literature when confronted by disaster on such a massive scale as is found in global war, the ubiquity of lust and fear, the lonely impotence and anguish of the intellectual with a social conscience and fading political hopes. And while he analyses his thoughts and feelings he communicates a powerful physical sense of what service life was really like, the boozing, the tawdriness and sentimentality of the popular arts, the well-meaning stupidity and intolerance of his comrades, the discomfort, boredom and frustration.

The first sonnet in the sequence describes a public bar which is suddenly flooded with music from a radio and Fuller suggests that this music may give permanence to the transitory moment and perishable object but, rather ambiguously, it seems that the stasis conferred upon the shifting and ephemeral by art is very close to the fixity of death. Here is the sestet:

> Not only these strange winter flowers take on
> In this dread air the meaning of a myth,
> But all the common objects now have gone
> Into the littoral which borders death.
> The ancient sailor holds an unplumbed glass;
> The girl is instantly a sculptured mass.

The second sonnet deals with the cinema which can 'stir a huge authentic feeling' and, though the word 'authentic' might surprise the reader who associated popular films with the emotionally meretricious, a moment's reflection should persuade him that it is used with accuracy, for however shoddy or gross by aesthetic standards the cause of the emotion there can be no doubting the reality of the feeling itself. In the third sonnet Fuller refers to '. . . the illusion of the word' and suggests that, finally, all art, all means of self-expression in the face of '. . . the epoch's tragedies' are inadequate. Sonnet IV continues the meditation on the hideous destructiveness of war and on the way in which those involved grow indifferent to the fate of others:

The morning sheet emphatically is leaded
With news of cities gone—and left unread.

The newspaper is a thing for carrying death, a winding sheet, and the type is 'leaded' like a coffin, but it no longer has the power to disturb. It is ignored as:

The years of war pile on our heads like lime,
And horrors grow impersonal as engines;
Nor can I think in discipline and slime.
Perhaps beside some blue and neutral lake
Another Lenin sorts the real from fake.

The reference to Lenin, who wrote his most important work, *Imperialism,* when exiled in peaceful Switzerland, suggests that such a vantage point of detachment is necessary for a just assessment of the rights and wrongs of a situation like the war, but detachment is not possible for the man in uniform as the next poem in the sequence makes clear with its evocation of barrack-square life in sharp and memorable images:

Day after day upon the concrete square,
Cargo for sinking iron, sweaty places,
The men assemble with their cold, cramped
                                        faces.

The sestet starts with these lines:

Now man must be political or die;
Nor is there really that alternative.
Correctly to be dedicated and to live
By chance, is what the species asks.

Fuller is saying here that, in time of war and especially for those serving in one or other of the armed forces, no man can isolate himself, either physically or mentally, from the calamity in which everyone is involved, and individual interests must be subordinated to the needs of the unit or state, that the necessary simplification of moral issues demands a common consent on matters of conduct or principle. And it seems almost certain that the poet is using the word 'political' with an awareness of its secondary meaning of 'expedient' or even 'crafty'.

The next sonnet takes us into the barrack-room where three men are conducting one of those argumentative conversations that everyone who served in any of the forces will remember, and their stupidity, prejudice and ignorance show them to be slaves of their education, environment and personal limitations and, especially, prisoners trapped by their present situation.

> 'The strikers should be shot,' one says: his
> hand
> A craftsman's, capable and rough. The second:
> 'Niggers and Jews I hate.' It is the squawking
> Of an obscene and guiltless bird. They sit,
> Free men, in prison. And the third: 'I hate
> Nobody'—raising, to gesticulate,
> His arm in navy with a gun on it.

The last three sonnets restate Fuller's melancholy conviction that while history is being made those who are its manufacturers are quite ignorant of their part in the process and are concerned only with personal survival, and that art, philosophy, the life of the intellect and imagination become trivial beside the atrocious reality of war, and, finally, he acknowledges his guilt for his failure as a sensitive and educated intellectual, who would claim to be concerned about his fellow men, to do anything for them at all.

> Their weakness is the measure of
> My own, their guilt my own inactive past;
> Their stormy future mine, who wish that love

Could melt the guns, expropriate a caste.
How, when my only rank is consciousness,
Can I despise them, far less pity, bless?

I cannot regard *Winter in Camp* as an unqualified success. It is needlessly repetitive and some of its parts are better than others (Sonnet VII, for instance, is confused and confusing in its sestet) but it does clearly show Fuller's main strength, his honesty and steadfast refusal to try to impress the reader by sleight of mind or rhetorical extravagance. At a time when the crabbed and quasi-gnomic are fashionable it is refreshing to return to the work of a poet who takes more risks than a superficial reading might lead one to believe: he risks making undisguised statements about his responses to an experience which is both personal and general; he is not afraid to be explicit and he is justified in having confidence in a mind which is always lively and original enough to give his readers pleasure. His imagery seldom strays far from the concrete and particular so that his poems, at their best, have a solidity and strength which guarantee longevity. For the consistency, quality and quantity of his wartime verse Roy Fuller must be rated as one of the best poets of the 1939–45 war.

Alan Ross and Charles Causley

The four poets dealt with in the preceding chapters are the ones who instantly come to my mind when I am asked, as I am with deplorable frequency, 'Second World War poets? *Were* there any?'; but there were many other skillful and serious writers producing poetry of lasting value, some of whom have gone on to establish large reputations with their post-war work, others who have remained silent or suffered almost total neglect. Alan Ross and Charles Causley have both continued to publish collections of verse fairly regularly and both have received some specialist and popular recognition, though Ross, it seems to me, has been given less than his due; both served during the war in the Royal Navy and, unlike Roy Fuller, they both experienced combat and, in the case of Alan Ross, a great deal of it.

Ross joined the Navy in 1942, coming straight from Oxford at the age of twenty. He served as an Ordinary Seaman in destroyers and minesweepers, was later commissioned and continued to sail in ships that were actively engaged in fighting the war. He has written:

'The Navy—at least when one was at sea—was ideal for writing, once you got used to the noise and complete lack of privacy. Also for reading: I think I must have read and reread between 1942 and 1945 almost every volume of poetry published since Eliot's first book, hundreds of American novels, the complete works of D. H. Lawrence, Forster, Isherwood, Green and Greene among others.

'I felt a week was wasted that produced no poem. Out of a hundred or so I've kept a dozen, though many others appeared in magazines. The issues of the war seemed to me clear beyond all ambiguity, therefore one could concentrate on recording a kind of existence as accurately as possible. I had no particular ties, no important relationships, so deprivation or separation were not the motivating impulses they were for others, and have since been for me. I found the sea beautiful and life in a warship rich and rewarding. I hoped to survive, so that I could live the romance I had read about. That's about all there was to it, though since there was virtually no sea-war poetry in either war I found making my own poems unusually difficult. Had the war come a bit later I might have been able to do better by it.'

In fact, considering his youth at the time, Alan Ross did remarkably well by the war at sea, and the dozen war poems which he has preseved in *Poems 1942–67* are all, in their different ways, viable pieces of work, and they show how he succeeded in finding a style which could handle both the violence and confusion of sea battle and the less dramatic material of day-to-day life at sea or stationed on shore. The first two poems of the twelve are decidedly romantic in tone and the language seems to owe something to the nineties' 'decadents', Dowson or Francis Thompson. *Leave Train* begins:

> Yellow as daffodils as wax fingers
> Yellow as death as a mandarin
> Rosyth with eyes like a stranger
> Rosyth with the pallor of dawn.

and you feel that the immediate scene is being observed through the spectacles of a literary past. The same second-hand romanticism weakens *Morning Watch*:

> These black ships and welts
> Of saffron streaking our mess,

> Crate up and cradle all we possess,
> Sunroses strewn over white horses.

But in the third poem, *Messdeck*, Ross confronts the realities of the situation squarely and presents the physical images with clarity, allowing them to make their own statement rather in the way that the best of the Second World War official artists reflected the texture of life in air-raid shelter, camp, barrack-room and on the lower deck. There are no *fin de siècle* languours here; both image and diction are exact and the sprung rhythms of the loosely constructed sonnet supply an appropriately heaving, sea-like music:

> The bulkhead sweating, and under naked bulbs
> Men writing letters, playing ludo. The light
> Cuts their arms off at the wrist, only the dice
> Lives. Hammocks swing, nuzzling in tight
> Like foals into flanks of mares. Bare shoulders
> Glisten with oil, tattoo-marks rippling their
>   scales on
> Mermaids or girls' thighs as dice are shaken,
>   cards played.
> We reach for sleep like a gas, randy for
>   oblivion.
> But, laid out on lockers, some get waylaid;
> And lie stiff, running off films in the mind's
>   dark-room.
> The air soupy, yet still cold, a beam sea rattles
> Cups smelling of stale tea, knocks over a
>   broom.
> The light is watery, like the light of the sea-
>   bed.
> Marooned in it, stealthy as fishes, we may
>   even be dead.

Destroyers in the Arctic continues to explore the style of *Messdeck*, this time in rhyming couplets with a flowing rhythm which never moves far away from the cadences of normal speech but is sufficiently disciplined and aware of itself as never to become prosaic.

Camouflaged, they detach lengths of sea and
               sky
When they move; offset, speed and directions
               are a lie.

Everything is grey anyway, ships, water,
               snow, faces.
Flanking the convoy, we rarely go through
               our paces.

But sometimes on tightening waves at night
               they wheel
Drawing white moons on strings from
               dripping keel.

Cold cases them, like ships in glass, they are
               formal,
Not real, except in adversity. Such deception
               is normal.

At dusk they intensify dusk, strung out, non-
               committal:
Waves spill from our wake, crêpe paper
               magnetised by gun-metal.

The poem ends with the destroyers in port:

. . . . We dream we are counterfeits tied to our
               jetty.

But cannot dream long, the sea curdles and
               sprawls,

Liverishly real, horizon and water tilting in to
                                    walls.

This is very good descriptive verse, and the same qualities of control, observation and the power to translate what is observed in sharp visual images are shown in the next two poems, *Iceland in Winter* and *Night Patrol*, but one becomes aware of something lacking: the skill is admirable, especially from such a young poet, but the reticence, the cool, appraising eye, the lack of personal involvement leave one a little unsatisfied. Things happen in the poems but they seem to happen autonomously, without human aid or interference.

Docks dwindle, rubbed out by mists,
Their cranes, like drunks, askew
Over jetties. Coal is unloaded
Under blue arc-lights.

Those lines are from *Night Patrol* which ends:

We're on our own, making for harbour.
In tangerine light we sniff greenness,
Tremble like racehorses. Soon minesweepers
Pass us, continuing our business.

Now, while one relishes the confident movement of the verse, the nicety of observation, this pleasure is diluted by the realisation that nothing has been said about the men themselves, what they felt and thought, some very attractive images have been presented but the reader is no wiser than before as to what it feels like to be on a night patrol in a destroyer during the war.

The next poem, *Survivors*, is compelled by its subject to deal with the human and it does so very effectively and, incidentally, shows that the fact that '. . . there was virtually no sea-poetry in either war . . .' was not a real obstacle to the writing of poems of nautical action at all and that the techniques employed by the best of the soldier poets in the First World War and by the politically committed poets of the thirties were perfectly adequate for the sailor's purposes in the Second World War. While it is unmistakably post-1914–18 in tone, the laconic conversational voice, the irregularly placed mixture of rhymes and near-rhymes—it is also quite close to Sassoon and Owen:

> But soon they joke, easy and warm,
> As men will who have died once
> Yet somehow were able to find their way—
> Muttering this was not included in their pay.
>
> Later, sleepless at night, the brain spinning
> With cracked images, they won't forget
> The confusion and the oily dead,
> Nor yet the casual knack of living.

In *Naval Base*, too, there is a marked involvement in the human experience of war, a recording of the continuous awareness among servicemen who are, or have been, directly concerned with the fighting, of the likelihood of sudden and violent death, their own or that of their comrades.

> Waiting in the bar for the war to end—
> Those who for the second time saw it begin
> And, charting the future, watch death crawling
> Like a lizard over the lidless eyes of the sun
> And the leprous face of the coast being eaten
> Away by the sea—the glass shows them now
> The face and features that they find appalling.

Then, in the next poem, *Radar,* we find Ross considering the impersonal and mechanical nature of so much of the killing in modern warfare and the way in which the operators of equipment, which by itself has no destructive power, will work in

co-operation with those who control the killing apparatus—
the guns, depth-charges and so on—with the result that the
responsibility for taking life and the consequent guilt is divided
and apparently reduced by being shared or, at least, made
easier to evade.

> Control is remote, feelings, like hands,
> Gloved by space. Responsibility is shared, too.
> And destroying the enemy by radar
> We never see what we do.

This is really the first evidence of a moral awareness of the
complexities and ambiguities of the role of the killer in war
that Ross's poetry shows, and the broadening and refining of
his responses to the experience of being a man at war are further
demonstrated in *Night Train Images* with no loss of the power to
create atmosphere and the sense of an exact place that he showed
from the start. There are weaknesses in the poem: the lines
'The airless carriage sweats through loosened dress, / Our faces
sag in flesh that never basks.' are spoilt by the uncharacteristically awkward and imprecise 'basks' which has obviously been
forced in by the need to rhyme with 'gas-masks' which ends an
earlier line, but the first section ends confidently and communicates a real sense of the event:

> The train takes you where you have to go.
>
> Outside, Lincolnshire is deliberate with
>   aerodromes;
> Passengers are forced to become their own
>   homes.
>
> The carriage jolts, the lemon light unfolds a
>   bed
> Whose occupants still sleep or appear dead.
>
> But now look up, half nod and mask a yawn;

Night grows soft with rain and streaks of
                                        dawn.

The train takes you where you have to go.

The second and final section consists of just two quatrains in a different metre from the first and there is a shift in viewpoint from that which sees the passengers in the wartime train as being the victims of a necessity from which they are powerless to escape, except into fantasy, to the recognition that, despite the apparent uniformity of response and behaviour that service life imposes on the individual, unique identities are still there beneath the conforming disguises; and here again a weak line, the last of the poem, seems to have been dictated by the need for a rhyme, this time for that notorious forcer of bad rhymes, 'love'.

The uniforms conceal identity, make
Conversation the exchange of counters,
Though experience helps us now to fake
Responses in our false encounters.

The make-up glistens on a face,
The look might be of lust or love;
But opposite the mirror shows
The leopard speaking through the dove.

Presumably Ross means to suggest that the true, undissembling responses will in careless moments reveal themselves to the impartial observer—or, unawares be betrayed by the mirror— but surely the leopard is too strong, too melodramatic an emblem for what I take to be the ordinary human hunger and selfishness that is actually there, and the dove has been for too long established as a symbol of the abstraction of peace to be used to image a human quality or facial expression.

In *A Letter from the Sea* the first person singular is employed and for the first time the poet's private feelings and attitudes are

directly expressed in loose rhyming couplets which are written
with dexterity and some rhythmic invention and carry the
ruminative, conversational tone without noticeable contrivance.
This style probably owes something to Auden's letter-poems but
I think I detect echoes from an earlier poet, Siegfried Sassoon:

> . . . . But both have come through
> The Dardanelles of fear, I imagine, without
> > new
> Illusions, only able a little better
> To make judgements. My letter,
> However, was not for this, but talking
> To you again is like walking
> After a long illness, and I had meant,
> As against the handrail I leaned
> Staring while the wake uncoiled
> The foamed wash of sunset and sea boiled
> Away under our screws—
> At least to send you wishes, give you news.

And later in the poem there is a feeling of tightly reined emotion
which, if unchecked, might burst into an unmanly or ungentle-
manly display of sentiment and this again reminds me of
Sassoon:

> We've had, I fear, our losses, but I won't
> Write you of them. They don't
> In any case stand reminiscence, what's over,
> As from the desert you well know, is over.
> But the funerals at sea, with guns
> Firing as each neatly-sewed body runs
> Gently over the side, and the sea seems
> Respectfully to make way, will return in dreams
> For most of us, bringing quick tears to eyes,
> Which for their sake we shall not despise.

We find then in the dozen war poems that Ross has chosen to

preserve a steady development and widening of range from late nineteenth-century picturesque romanticism and 'literariness', through impersonal, almost photographic realism to a poetry which is both personal and general, and it is in the last of these poems, *J.W.51B A Convoy*, that he makes an ambitious attempt at writing a big poem on naval warfare in which his talent for sharp visual imagery, his rhythmic resourcefulness and his first-hand experience of battle at sea are fused to create a work which might stand as a monument to the historical event and to the men with whom he served and the qualities they embodied. For a poet in his early twenties it is a most impressive achievement: over five hundred lines composed in a variety of metres, free verse, rhyme and half-rhyme, full of excellent local effects and given an overall authority by close familiarity with the technicalities of fighting at sea and an accurate ear for the idiom of the lower deck.

An epigraph to the poem supplies the plot:

From the *Supplement* to the *London Gazette*, 17 October 1950: 'The conduct of all officers and men of the escort and covering forces throughout this successful action against greatly superior forces was in accordance with the traditions of the service. That an enemy force of at least one pocket battleship, one heavy cruiser and six destroyers, with all the advantages of surprise and concentration, should be held off for four hours by five destroyers and driven from the area by two 6-inch cruisers, without any loss to the convoy, is most creditable and satisfactory.'

The poem opens with a short passage in free, unrhymed verse which economically supplies the necessary information, sets the scene and introduces some of the ratings on the *Onslow*, one of six destroyers escorting the merchantmen carrying tanks, stores and artillery from Scapa to Murmansk. The voyage begins late on Christmas Eve:

> At 2300, when at home trees were being
> Laden with presents and last year's Father
>   Christmas

Was buttoning his duffle and seeing
Beyond the mineswept channel that one face
Warm on a pillow that trailed
Hair through dreams of reunion, they sailed,
Line abreast and making thirteen knots . . . .

Then we meet more of the men who serve on the *Onslow,* are
shown their special characteristics and idiosyncracies, and we
see how the crew, each member a unique individual with his
own peculiarities, dreams and obsessions, is also a corporate
body and only mutual tolerance, sympathy and a form of love
can keep that body functioning and whole. The first part of the
poem ends:

Courses crossing, like lines on a hand,
Darkness disintegrating, and throwing up
Into the net of the morning, like fish,
A stranded sea of vessels, ignorantly
Approaching, British and German.

The *Onslow* engages the enemy cruiser, *Hipper,* and in the
exchange the British destroyer is hit and set on fire. The scenes
of action are well described with vivid and entirely functional
visual effects like the 'bridges' simile in these lines:

. . . . while he himself
Went after *Hipper,* peppering her,
Tracers like bridges of fireworks
Linking over distance, and the slow
Grey swell heaving itself up,
Collapsing and breathless.

Or the picture of the snowfall:

Herringbone waters, and the cold
Drifting south, narrowing

The escape routes, icing breeches,
A slow confetti of snow
Made bridal the gun teams . . . .

Or the death of the wireless operator:

'A' and 'B' Guns unable to fire,
Radar destroyed, aerials ripped,
And, forward, the sea stripping
The Mess decks, spilling over tables,
Fire and water clinching like boxers
As the ship listed, sprawling them.
Tamblin, his earphones awry, like a laurel
                                        wreath
Slipped on a drunken god, gargled to death
In water with a noise of snoring.

The fire is extinguished and *Onslow*, whose captain has been wounded, has the temerity to engage another German cruiser and even forces it to withdraw. After the battle the convoy proceeds on its way:

From snow into snow. A kind
Of deliverance, an unloading.
As skies, snow-heavy, are lightened
By the falling of flakes, the mind
Also is eased of anxieties.
The rattle of anchors, whiff of fish,
And Lyons, after a run ashore,
Tucking in the ears of his Rabbits,
Or so he imagined himself,
Gazing at low hills like snow-clouds,
And snow-clouds like low hills.

Arrived, the deck stationary, bulkheads
                                    sweating.

This poem is, by any standards, an impressive and original piece of writing. The narrative grips hard, there is a satisfying shape to the work and the language slips from the colloquial to the lyrical or impersonal descriptive with fluent ease. I may be mistaken in thinking that the movement of the verse has been influenced, consciously or unconsciously, by that great English poem of the sea, *The Wreck of the Deutschland,* but certainly I find my ear more than once being reminded of Hopkins:

> He saw, the convoy steaming sedate
> As swans on a river, his own ship
> Flying pennants of smoke,
> *Obedient* and *Orwell* and *Obdurate*
> To port, from time to time
> Making sorties on a horizon
> Of gunflash, returning to the rhyme
> Of escort after passages of free verse.

> Beneath the ice-floes sleeping,
> Embalmed in salt
> The sewn-up bodies slipping
> Into silent vaults.
> The sea of Barents received them,
> Men with no faults
> Of courage, for the weeping
> Would be elsewhere,
> Far from its keeping.

Of course, the stanzas in *The Wreck of the Deutschland* are more highly organised and the resemblance in tone may be an accidental one, something to do with Ross's fairly frequent use of sprung rhythm, but I do not think I am mistaken in hearing echoes, however faint, of:

> Into the snow she sweeps,
> Hurling the haven behind,

The Deutschland, on Sunday, and so the
sky keeps,
For the infinite air is unkind,
And the sea flint-flake, black-backed in the
regular blow,
Sitting Eastnortheast, in cursed quarter, the
wind,
Wiry and white-fiery and whirlwind-
swivelled snow
Spins to the widow-making unchilding
unfathering deeps.

Whatever his influences were, Alan Ross produced some very good poems from his life in the Royal Navy and it is past the time for his achievement to be more widely acclaimed.

Charles Causley's poetry, distilled from his life in the Royal Navy during the Second World War, is very different from that of both Alan Ross and Roy Fuller. As we have seen, Fuller, although totally committed to the political left, to an ideal of social justice and to effecting a break-down of the existing class-structure, was a middle-class intellectual and something of a solitary who did not feel at ease among men from working-class backgrounds whose notions of the good life were vastly different from his own, and his progress from lower deck to commissioned rank and an administrative job seemed inevitable. Ross also began his service as a rating but he, too, soon became an officer and one feels that such was his natural role. There is something cool and detached about much of his verse; emotion is there, of course, but it is tightly reined and no more of it is displayed than is commensurate with good form. Causley, on the other hand, was of working-class origins and he seemed to have accepted the lower deck as his rightful place of habitation. There is nothing overtly political in his wartime poetry, which is much more romantic, 'poetical', 'inspired' than either of the other naval poets, and there is no attempt to capture the mood of the period, no sense of rationed, blacked-out, anxious, battle-

dressed, despoiled Britain in time of war. The low-keyed
realism which had been the prevailing style of the younger
thirties poets and which had proved itself in the hands of
Fuller and others able to deal with the experience of total war
was almost completely eschewed by Causley whose characteristic tone is dream-like, lyrical and richly coloured and whose
poems tend towards a transmutation of the immediate and
actual into something timeless and mythical. Yet he, more than
any other serious poet of the time, came close to producing a
genuinely popular poetry, work which could be enjoyed by
people from widely differing social and educational environ-
ments and of different levels of intellectual capacity and aesthetic
sophistication. And he could create such a poetry without any
dilution of his poetic intentions and integrity.

Much of Causley's best work is composed in traditional
verse-forms employing conventional metres and regular
rhyme-patterns, and he has an especial liking for the ballad or
forms closely related to it, but he usually contrives, with
considerable deftness, to avoid sounding archaic or uncomfortably artificial through the freshness and contemporaneity of
much of his language and imagery, through the vigour of his
rhythms and a judicicious spicing of wit. The Auden of *Miss Gee*
and *Victor* and some of Betjeman have struck a similar note and
one feels that A. E. Housman, Walter de la Mare, Kipling and
probably Chesterton, as well as the English, Irish and Scottish
ballads collected by Quiller-Couch in *The Oxford Book of Ballads*
have been of value to Causley in the forging of his style:

> As I walked down by the river
> Down by the frozen fen
> I saw the grey cathedral
> With the eyes of a child of ten.
> O the railway arch is smoky
> As the Flying Scot goes by
> And but for the Education Act
> Go Jumper Cross and I.
>
> But war is a bitter bugle
> That all must learn to blow

And it didn't take long to stop the song
In the dirty Italian snow.
O war is a casual mistress
And the world is her double bed
She has few charms in her mechanised arms
But you wake up and find yourself dead.

The olive tree in winter
Casts her banner down
And the priest in white and scarlet
Comes up from the muddy town.
O never more will Jumper
Watch the Flying Scot go by
His funeral knell was a six-inch shell
Singing across the sky.

(From *A Ballad for Katherine of Aragon*)

Death is always dealt with by Causely in a euphemistic way: it is
a silencer of song or, as in *Song of the Dying Gunner A.A.1*, its
claws are drawn both by the music and by the imagery which
denies death's ugliness and finality through a vague literary
pantheism:

Oh mother my mouth is full of stars
As cartridges in the tray
My blood is a twin-branched scarlet tree
And it runs all away.

Oh *Cooks to the Galley* is sounded off
And the lads are down in the mess
But I lie done by the forward gun
With a bullet in my breast.

This is very attractive stuff but the real presence of death seems
far removed.

In *H.M.S. Glory* an aircraft-carrier is anthropomorphised and
it describes its own origins and memories in the first person,

opening in what might seem to be a manner closer to the realism
of the thirties:

> I was born on an Irish sea of eggs and porter,
> I was born in Belfast, in the MacNeice country,
> A child of Harland & Wolff in the iron forest,
> My childbed a steel cradle slung from a
> > gantry.
>
> I remember the Queen's Road trams swarming
> > with workers,
> The lovely northern voices, the faces of the
> > women,
> The plane trees by the City Hall: an
> > *Alexanderplatz,*
> And the sailors coming off shore with silk
> > stockings and linen.

But again there is a softness here, a romantic veil which obscures
or blurs and colours the iron-hard reality, and the essential
fancifulness of the poem is confirmed by the last two lines and
the appearance of that most literary of creatures, the albatross:

> Turning my face from home to the Southern
> > Cross,
> A map of crackling stars, and the albatross.

H.M.S. Glory at Sydney starts with unabashed romanticism:

> *Now it seems an old forgotten fable:*
> *The snow-goose descending on the still lagoon,*
> *The trees of summer flowering ice and fire*
> *And the sun coming up on the Blue Mountains.*

This poem was evidently written after the war and it is filled with nostalgia for a time and place and circumstance which will never be revisited. It is composed in fairly loose free verse and it shows that when Causley abandons the formal dancing-steps of prescribed metre he is apt at times to stumble and wander. Still, it is an amiable, slightly sentimental and very colourful tribute to the town of Sydney as remembered by a wartime matelot and the fact that temporal distance has lent enchantment to his view does not mean that the poem is a falsification of experience, for the experience being recorded here is not the immediate reality but its later, idealised recollection.

One of the few poems of realistic direct observation in his first collection, in which his wartime poems were published, *Farewell, Aggie Weston,* is also written in free verse, handled more confidently than in *H.M.S. Glory at Sydney,* doubtless lent control by the necessity of focusing on its single subject. This poem, *Chief Petty Officer,* is a fine and accurate portrait of a human type, it is witty without patronage, sharply observed but without malice. The first two lines ironically echo Pater's famous description of the Mona Lisa which begins: 'She is older than the rocks among which she sits . . .'

> He is older than the naval side of British
> history.
> And sits
> More permanent than the spider in the
> enormous wall.
> His barefoot, coal-burning soul,
> Expands, puffs like a toad, in the convict air
> Of the Royal Naval Barracks at Devonport.

The man is at once formidable and absurd:

> He has the face of the dinosaur
> That sometimes stares from old Victorian
> naval photographs:
> That of some elderly lieutenant
> With boots and a celluloid Crippen collar,

Brass buttons and cruel ambitious eyes of
                              almond.

He was probably made a Freemason in Hong
                              Kong.
He has a son (on War Work) in the Dockyard,
And an appalling daughter
In the W.R.N.S.
He writes on your draft-chit,
Tobacco-permit or request-form
In a huge antique Borstal hand,
And pins notices on the board in the Chiefs'
                              Mess
Requesting his messmates not to
Lay on the billiard table.
He is an anti-Semite and has somewhat
                      reactionary views,
And reads the pictures in the daily news.

Causley makes no explicit judgement but fixes his subject neatly and permanently:

A whole war later
He will still be sitting under a pusser's clock
Waiting for tot-time,
His narrow forehead ruffled by the Jutland
                              wind.

But the directness and immediacy of *Chief Petty Officer,* its objectivity, are not to be found in Causley's other wartime poems, which, instead of exploring and recording the bitter realities of lower-deck service in time of war, the boredom, physical discomfort, lack of privacy, fear, violence and claustrophobia, seem more concerned with transforming and idealising, consciously making literature from carefully selected parts of his experience as a sailor. For example, the language and imagery of both *H.M.S. Eclipse Approaches Freetown* and *Convoy* have a softness, brightness and sweetness, even a cosiness, that offer palliatives against the abrasiveness of the realities they disguise.

> I sing of the keen destroyer
> Ranging on the silken doors of the morning,
> Cutting through the panels of the South
> > > > Atlantic:
> Strands of light streaming in the steel rigging.
> And the warning:
> The yellow stammer from the lighthouse of
> > > > white sugar
> Pales as the African sun unfolds her tail of
> > > > golden peacock
> Over the fevered harbour.

Elizabethan Sailor's Song is a pretty piece of pastiche without the allegorical relevance of *Nursery Rhyme of Innocence and Experience* and even in the less formal, ostensibly more direct and colloquial poems like *Conversation in Gibralter* and *Demobilisation Leave* seem more concerned with history, art and literature than with the experiences the verses purport to be handling.

> We sit here, talking of Barea and Lorca,
> Meeting the iron eye of the Spanish clock.
> We have cut, with steel bows, the jungle of
> > > > salt-water,
> Sustaining the variable sea-fevers of home and
> > > > women,
> To walk the blazing ravine
> Of the profitable Rock.
>
> We hold, in our pockets, no comfortable
> > > > return tickets:
> Only the future, gaping like some hideous
> > > > fable
> The antique Mediterranean of history and
> > > > Alexander,

The rattling galley and the young Greek
                                captains
Are swept up and piled
Under the table.

> (From: *Conversation in Gibralter*)

I have seen the white tiger,
Imagination,
In the Douanier Rousseau forest:
Isosceles leaves and a waterfall of compasses.
And although I am writing in Cornwall, in
                                winter,
And the rain is coming in from the moor,
Trincomali, ah Trincomali!
The Technicolour market, the monkeys and
                                chickens.
The painted boats at Vegetable Jetty . . . .

> (From: *Demobilisation Leave*)

Every poem in *Farewell, Aggie Weston* has its appeal and Causley is never dull, but, as war poems, they generally contrive to evade direct confrontation with the material with which most war poetry deals, actual violence, terror, loneliness, separation and death. The quality that his poems all possess is the rather incongruous one of charm, but this is not to disparage Causley, for to write such work, under such circumstances—much of it, of its kind, excellent—is a remarkable feat, and his contribution to the literature of the Second World War adds to its richness and variety.

Henry Reed and Others

It is a curious fact that what is probably the most widely quoted and anthologised single poem written in the Second World War came from the pen of some one who served only a few months in the Army before being released to work at the Foreign Office. This poem, by Henry Reed, is called *Naming of Parts* and it is the first in a sequence entitled *Lessons of the War*. Reed was a war poet only in the sense that he wore uniform and underwent military training and without that experience he would not have been able to write the three *Lessons of the War* (subsequent sections were added to this group of poems long after hostilities had ended, but with these we are not here concerned). He saw no combat as a soldier and he was not interested in the problems that Douglas, Lewis, and Ross in their different ways attempted to solve, those of communicating the sense of what it was like to serve in foreign lands, facing imminent and violent death, and of articulating the longings, anxieties and frustrations of the fighting serviceman in statements that were at once subjective and self-exploratory yet representative of the spirit of a generation.

All true poets are, of course, primarily concerned with the artefact, the making of a verbal construct, a durable work of art, but some are more deeply involved than others in the raw experience which lies behind the poem and for them the act of composition is an act of self-exploration with the definite goal of enlightenment rather than the ideally depersonalised construction of a beautiful and autonomous object. W. H. Auden has written in his essay on Walter de la Mare: 'One might say that, in every poet, there dwells an Ariel, who sings, and a Prospero, who comprehends, but in any particular poem, sometimes even in the whole work of a particular poet, one of the partners plays a greater role than the other.' Henry Reed, compared with the writers I mentioned, is an Ariel-dominated poet whose main interest in the writing of a poem is one of aesthetics and craft and whose concern with probing into the reality in which the poem originated is secondary. It might therefore seem strange that he should have written one of the most memorable poems of the war and, indeed, there was something almost accidental about the way this work became the most complete and poignant articulation we have of the consciousness of the reluctant conscript, the alienated, sensitive soldier-in-uniform enduring a hateful but necessary process aimed at changing his very nature.

Henry Reed has said[30] that, during the war, he would entertain his friends by giving a comic imitation of a sergeant-instructor and, after a few performances, he came to notice that the utterances of the N.C.O., couched in the style of the military manual, fell into certain rhythmic patterns which fascinated him and which supplied the foundation for the structure of *Naming of Parts*. The cunningly placed rhythmic pauses, the edgy, short sense-units in the earlier lines of each stanza echo the mechanical rhetoric of the sergeant-instructor and, with no feeling of dislocation, they are able to modulate into the more flowing, lyrical passage that follows. Each of the six-line stanzas is contrapuntal in both mood and rhythm, and the two voices— the decidedly audible one of the N.C.O., and the sub-vocal, meditative one of the trainee—are entirely convincing at a realistic level, perfectly counterpointed artistically, and they represent, too, the divided self of the gentle, creative man compelled to adopt the role of the fighter.

I have remarked before on that pervasive and ubiquitous mist of sexual longing and deprivation that was part of the air one breathed in the atmosphere of barracks, camp and ship during the war, and, in *Naming of Parts,* Reed insinuates a thread of sexual innuendo into the punning which is integral to the poem's scheme and its singular richness, a thread which first appears in the title itself and becomes unequivocal in the third and fourth stanzas:

This is the safety-catch, which is always
                      released
With an easy flick of the thumb. And please do
                      not let me
See anyone using his finger. You can do it
                      quite easy
If you have any strength in your thumb. The
                      blossoms
Are fragile and motionless, never letting
                      anyone see
Any of them using their finger.

And this you can see is the bolt, The purpose
                      of this
Is to open the breech, as you see. We can
                      slide it
Rapidly backwards and forwards: we call this
Easing the spring. And rapidly backwards and
                      forwards
The early bees are assaulting and fumbling the
                      flowers:
They call it easing the Spring.

Naming of Parts ends where it began, with the formal intro-
ductory phrase of the instructor: '. . . today we have naming of
parts' and the stanza is a kind of coda in which the strands of
meaning and double meaning are woven together and the
principal theme is restated, the recognition of the power of
military training and the semi-monastic conditions of army life
to dehumanise and change the imaginative and creative man into
something almost as impersonally destructive as a rifle.

They call it easing the Spring: it is perfectly
                      easy
If you have any strength in your thumb: like
                      the bolt,
And the breech, and the cocking-piece, and the
                      point of balance,

Which in our case we have not got, and the
                              almond-blossom
Silent in all of the gardens and the bees going
                              backwards and forwards,
For today we have naming of parts.

The movement of the verse, the verbal wit and the balance of
the vernacular and lyrical voices combine to make *Naming of
Parts* a poem of exceptional quality, but the danger with a work
so original and fully achieved is that further poems adopting the
same or similar form and strategy are almost certain to fall below
the standard set by the original, and the other two wartime
poems in the sequence,—*Judging Distances* and *Unarmed Combat*—
while undoubtedly accomplished pieces of work, have not the
inevitability and unassailable perfection of *Naming of Parts*. It is
noticeable that the two voices in *Judging Distances* are not
nearly so distinctly variegated as in *Naming of Parts*. Now, this
may be a deliberate choice on the part of the poet, for there is in
these three poems a development towards a more affirmative
stance or, at least, towards a greater measure of acceptance, so it
is possible, and even likely, that the closer similarity of syntax,
vocabulary and idiom in the two voices is intended to reflect the
partial metamorphosis of the civilian into the efficient soldier.
However that may be, the complete authenticity of the N.C.O.'s
voice in *Naming of Parts* has given way to a more ambiguous
tone and one which sometimes carries a distinctly artificial,
literary, even a quasi-philosophical note in phrases like '. . . maps
are of time, not place', '. . . things only seem to be things', and
becomes almost arch in stanza three: '. . . where sheep may be
safely grazing'.

It might be argued that this idiomatic difference could be
accounted for by a difference in the rank of the instructor, that
in *Judging Distances* an officer of superior intelligence and education has taken over from the N.C.O., in *Naming of Parts,* but in
that case he would not say, as he does in the third stanza:

        . . . . You must say, when reporting:
At five o'clock in the central sector is a
                              dozen

> Of what appear to be animals, whatever you
> > do,
> > Don't call the bleeders *sheep*.

'Bleeders', unlike many profanities in demotic English, is peculiarly lower class and could hardly be uttered except with a Cockney accent.

There is another comparative weakness in *Judging Distances*. When the shift comes from the instructor's voice to the meditative, interior one of the recruit, the lyricism seems rather forced, and the rumination of the conscript a shade self-conscious, even self-congratulatory:

> I am sure that's quite clear, and suppose, for
> > the sake of example,
> The one at the end, asleep, endeavours to tell
> > us
> What he sees over there to the west, and how
> > far away,
> At first having come to attention. There to the
> > west,
> On the fields of summer the sun and the
> > shadows bestow
> > Vestments of purple and gold.

In *Unarmed Combat* the ambiguity of tone and attitude is even more pronounced and the poem's ironies are nervous, as if not quite sure of their ground. The voice of the instructor, which speaks through the first half of the poem, is still less differentiated in tone and syntax from the soliloquising voice of the recruit and there are no contrapuntal lyrical passages. I gather that this is meant to suggest that the soldier-civilian is becoming less distinguishable from his teacher and exemplar than in the earlier stages of his training and the final stanza essays a muted clarion call, a claim to a small victory that I find highly equivocal. The first stanza shows an impersonal, stiff and clumsy voice, insensitive to both the music and meaning of language:

In due course of course you will all be issued
                    with
Your proper issue, but until tomorrow,
You can hardly be said to need it, and until
                 that time,
We shall have unarmed combat . . . .

In the second stanza the heavy-booted speech of the instructor continues and the metaphor of 'balance' is echoed from *Naming of Parts*; then the stiff-necked homily of stanzas three and four ends with a line that is reverberant enough to be picked up and developed by the meditative voice which takes over the rest of the poem:

So give them all you have, and always give
                   them
As good as you get, it will always get you
                 somewhere.
(You may not know it, but you can tie a Jerry
Up without a rope, it is one of the things I
              shall teach you.)
Nothing matters if only you are ready for him.
    The readiness is all.

But when the phrase is repeated and the whole lesson re-stated with an exploration of each instruction's metaphorical implications, a note of self-pity and one almost of self-parody obtrudes.

The readiness is all. How can I help but feel
I have been here before? But somehow then,
I was the tied-up one. How to get out
Was always then my problem. And even if I
                had
A piece of rope I was always the sort of
              person
    Who threw the rope aside.

And in my time I have given them all I had
Which was never as good as I got, and it got
                              me nowhere.
And the various holds and rolls and throws
                              and breakfalls
Somehow or other I always seemed to put
In the wrong place. And as for war, my wars
          Were global from the start

Stanza seven ends with the statement 'It is courage that counts' and then we come to the ambiguous conclusion of the poem:

Things may be the same again; and we must
                              fight
Not in the hope of winning but rather of
                              keeping
Something alive: so that when we meet our
                              end,
It may be said that we tackled wherever we
                              could,
That battle-fit we lived, and though defeated,
          Not without glory fought.

I find these lines ambiguous because the surface meaning, where the poet appears to have at least partly accepted the military ethic and the necessity for the subjugation of the contemplative, creative individual to the active and mindless destroyer, is contradicted by the tone, not only of this section alone but of the whole trilogy, and the paraphrase of his epigraph—*Vixi duellis nuper idoneus | Et militavi non sine gloria*—which ends *Unarmed Combat* surely carries overtones of irony. Reed's apparent resignation to historical necessity and the exigencies of time and circumstance, his acceptance of the martial role and his modest claim to some qualified success in it, is not altogether what it seems. The struggle which '. . . we must fight / Not in the hope of winning but rather of keeping / Something alive' is less the conflict with the Axis military forces than the poet's struggle to preserve his individuality and humanity against the depersonalising and mindless processes of army training and the enervating boredom of routine, and his principal weapons in this struggle are precisely those which are employed to such good effect in *Lessons of the War,* the weapons of intelligence, irony and a sense of balance.

If, as I suggested, Henry Reed is an Ariel-dominated poet, the war poetry of John Manifold (an Australian, born in Melbourne in 1915 who served in the Intelligence Corps in the Middle East and in France) is as clearly ruled by Prospero. This does not mean that Manifold is a slipshod writer with little regard for the intricacies of his craft any more than Reed's primary concern with form diminishes the intensity of his response to experience. But as a convinced revolutionary Marxist the Australian believes that poetry should affect the way in which people live and think and vote, and, although his vocabulary and idiom are of his own time and he shows signs of having read and profited from the work of Auden, his real affinities—at least in the satirical poems—seem to lie with the tough polemical verse-writers of the seventeenth and early eighteenth centuries. *A Hat in the Ring,* a satirical dialogue in rhymed couplets is intended to justify the value of the poet's function in society against arguments which deny him any practical usefulness at all. Manifold—or his spokesman, the poet—states:

> It has been said and will be said again,
> 'The typewriter is mightier than the Bren';
> Perhaps I have to emphasize for you
> First, that it scans, and second, that it's true.

This simplistic view of the nature of poetry seems to restrict his talent, especially in his committed political verse in which he becomes hectoring and—ironically since Roy Campbell was politically as far to the right as Manifold to the left—remarkably similar in tone to the South African's facile swagger and vulgar rhetoric:

> Guerilla words, the flying pasquinade,
> The slogan-epigram's stiletto blade,
> The loud Come-all-ye to a ballad air,
> The declamation in the crowded square,
> The spoken sonnet, eloquent and terse:
> These are the proper marks for adult verse;
> No job for 'wonder-children' but most fit
> To show Invention, Eloquence and Wit.
> And yield that best reward the poet needs—
> To know his Words result in worthy Deeds.

In *A Satire on Liberty*, written in 1945 as a kind of rhymed pamphlet exhorting the public to reject Tory lies and blandishments during the first post-war general election, the verse is pretty crude and its jaunty vigour and use of far-fetched Byronic rhymes are almost certainly inspired by Auden's *Letter to Lord Byron*, though Manifold lacks the 'Invention, Eloquence and Wit' that his model so abundantly possessed. It is in his sonnets that the Australian poet produces his best work and here something rather curious emerges. Of all the serious poets of the Second World War Manifold is closest to the earlier poets of the Great War—though for quite different reasons—in his total acceptance of the necessity to fight and to win, and in the high value he places upon comradeship, and in the contempt he expresses for those who will not fight. As a communist he saw the conflict as a stage in the progress towards the greater goal of a socialist Utopia and he sees in the clean functional economy of the weapons of war an example for the good soldier to emulate. In *Camouflage* he writes:

> Therefore if I must choose I prefer to sing
> The tommy gun, the clean, functional thing,
> The singlehander, deadly to the rigid line,
> Good at a job it doesn't attempt to conceal.

Give me time only to teach this hate of mine
The patience and integrity of the steel.

In *Oerlikon* (*Maritime A.A.*) he contrasts the menacing and
exact shapes of the anti-aircraft gun against the sea and sky
which form its background:

. . . . you know what they
                    have never
Been taught—matters of precise control,
                                clever
Positive knowledge—and justly value it.

And he approves the gun as a paradigm for men, who should
master the lessons of control and knowledge so that they can
perfect their environment.

We find in Manifold's work none of the tortured doubts and
conflicts which troubled Marxist intellectuals such as Roy
Fuller, who failed dismally to find a joyful sense of solidarity
with the working-class men he served with, for the Australian
seems to have been the kind of communist who commits
himself to his creed with the almost unquestioning zeal of a
religious fanatic, yet his best poems are far more than para-
phrases of the gospel according to St. Marx. In one of his most
effective sonnets, *The Sirens*, he refurbishes the ancient myth for
his own purpose without self-consciousness and with real style:

Odysseus heard the sirens; they were singing
Music by Wolf and Weinberger and Morley
About a region where the swans go winging,
Vines are in colour, girls are growing surely

Into nubility, and pylons bringing
Leisure and power to farms that live securely
Without a landlord. Still, his eyes were
                                stinging

With salt and sea-blink, and the ropes hurt
                                            sorely.

Odysseus saw the sirens; they were charming,
Blonde, with snub breasts and little neat
                                            posteriors,
But could not take his mind off the alarming

Weather report, his mutineers in irons,
The radio failing; it was bloody serious.
In twenty minutes he forgot the sirens.

His poem, *Recruits*, approves uncritically the way in which
service life insists upon the interests of the individual being
subordinated to the smooth functioning of the whole unit, and
he claims that, paradoxically, the individual becomes more and
not less valuable once he has accepted the necessity of surrender-
ing his sense of singular identity in favour of the community of
which he is a member.

What rescues the best of Manifold's work from the grey
ponderousness of most Marxist verse in the English language is
its author's style and sense of irony which he is prepared to
follow, even if it leads him into areas close to heresy. The
sonnet, *Ration Party*, for example, begins with a description of
men, urged on profanely by N.C.O.'s, labouring up a hill in the
pouring rain, carrying great burdens of stores and rations, and
their task is recognised as being heart-breakingly sisyphean:
'For all their toil serves only to replenish / Stores for tomorrow's
labours to begin.' But it is the sestet that carries the real irony
of the scene and it suggests wider historical and political
application:

Absurd to think that Liberty, the splendid
Nude of our dreams, the intercessory saint
For us to judgement, needs to be defended

By sick fatigue-men brimming with complaint
And misery, who bear till all is ended
Every imaginable pattern of restraint.

Perhaps Manifold's best-known war poem is the elegiac *The Tomb of Lt. John Learmonth, A.I.F.,* and here again we find a readiness to salute one of the older military virtues, that of pure physical courage, which is carried out with a directness and simplicity that is rare in Second World War literature. The poem is written in terza rima and, while it is occasionally weakened by careless phrasing and a little of the Roy Campbell type of bombast in the earlier parts, it is a touching tribute to a brave young Australian officer and poet who was killed in action in Crete, a boy of whom Manifold says:

> There was no word of hero in his plan;
> Verse should have been his love and peace his
> > trade,
> But history turned him to a partisan.

The concluding lines celebrate, with moving restraint, the young soldier's courage, 'chemically pure':

> I could as hardly make a moral fit
> Around it as around a lightning flash.
> There is no moral, that's the point of it,
>
> No moral. But I'm glad of this panache
> That sparkles, as from flint, from us and steel,
> True to no crown nor presidential sash
>
> Nor flag nor fame. Let others mourn and feel
> He died for nothing: nothings have their
> > place.
> While thus the kind and civilised conceal
>
> This spring of unsuspected inward grace
> And look on death as equals, I am filled
> With queer affection for the human race.

❋

During the Second World War, as in the 1914–18 conflict, a great number of young men in the fighting services, who were not poets at all, wrote verses because conditions of extreme adversity, fear, loneliness and deprivation often persuade people who would not otherwise dream of taking up the pen to attempt the making of poems. Some of these amateur writings found their way into print, usually in ephemeral magazines of the period, though occasionally to be preserved in hardier anthologies or even small volumes and, while they may offer something of interest to the historian of the times, I see nothing useful to be gained here by mentioning the names of the writers or giving details of their work. A very different case, though, is the quite considerable number of poets, not perhaps of great stature but honest competent craftsmen, who wrote serious poems from their experience of wearing the uniform of one or other of the fighting services and who, in some cases, produced work of a quality which many of those who survived the war were unable to recapture in time of peace.

Hamish Henderson, who served with the 51st Highland Division in the Middle East and in Europe, wrote one of the most ambitious poetic works to come out of the Second World War, *Elegies for the Dead in Cyrenaica*. In his foreword he writes:[31]

'These elegies and the Heroic Song in which they culminate were written between March 1943 and December 1947 in North Africa, in Italy and in Scotland. Four of them already existed in fragmentary form in the Autumn of 1942.

'It was the remark of a captured German officer which first suggested to me the theme of these poems. He had said: "Africa changes everything. In reality we are allies, and the desert is our common enemy."

'The troops confronting each other in Libya were relatively small in numbers. In the early stages of the desert war they were to a large extent forced to live off each other. Motor transport, equipment of all kinds and even armoured fighting vehicles changed hands frequently. The result was a curious "doppelgaenger" effect, and it is this, enhanced by the deceptive distances and uncertain directions of the North African wasteland, which I have tried to capture in some of the poems.

'After the African campaign had ended, the memory of this odd effect of mirage and looking-glass illusion persisted, and gradually became for me a symbol of our human civil war, in which the roles seem constantly to change and the objectives to shift and vary. It suggested too a complete reversal of the alignments and alliances which we had come to accept as inevitable. The conflict seemed rather to be between "the dead, the innocent"—that eternally wronged proletariat of levelling death in which all the fallen are comrades—and ourselves, the living, who cannot hope to expiate our survival but by "spanning history's apollyon chasm".'

I do not think that the poetry itself fulfills the expectations aroused by Henderson's foreword. He seems too strenuously determined to create a mythopoeic work—something on the scale of David Jones's *In Parenthesis* in the First World War—and, in aiming at the grand manner, he is sometimes afflicted by flatulence and his juxtapositions of the vernacular with the high style are not always successful. His main influences would seem to be Ezra Pound and Hugh Macdiarmid but he lacks the fine ear and verbal tact of his mentors at their best.

> The sons of man
> grow and go down in pain: they kneel for the
>   load
> and bow like brutes, in patience accepting the
>   burden,
> the pain fort and dour . . . Out of shuttered
>   Europe
> not even a shriek or a howl for its doomed
>   children
> is heard through the nihilist windvoice.

When he adopts a plain style, his language and imagery are usually undistinguished—'nervous fingers of searchlights'—and, in the second section of *Opening of an Offensive*, he breaks out in a painful rash of exaggerated Hopkinsese:

                    . . . . Confound
the damnable domination. Slake
the crashing breakers-húrled rúbble of the
                               guns.
Dithering darkness, we'll wake you! Héll's
                               bélls
blind you. Be broken, bleed
deathshead blackness!
          The thongs of the livid
firelights lick you
               jagg'd splinters rend you
                           underground
we'll bomb you, doom you, tomb you into
                     grave's mound

Nevertheless, *Elegies for the Dead in Cyrenaica* is far from being a negligible work and its sheer energy and seriousness command attention and respect. The Seventh Elegy, *Seven Good Germans* (they are good because, as the Tommy's truism has it, the only good German is a dead one) is finely judged and Henderson's sympathy for the enemy soldiers has a disciplined tenderness which keeps sentimentality at bay. The laconic closing lines, with the invocation of the German popular song, *Lili Marleen*, strike just the right note, hinting at the ordinariness, the sad vulgarity of the soldiers' deaths and lives, without losing sight of the pathos.

        Seven poor bastards
         dead in African deadland
    (tawny tousled hair under the issue blanket)
          wie einst Lili
        dead in African deadland
             einst Lili Marleen

Henderson does succeed in his *Elegies* in communicating to the reader what it was like to be an infantryman in the desert war and what it was like to wage war against the desert itself: the work has its moments of extravagance that sometimes verge on

the unintentionally comic but it is its passion and dignity that
finally stay in the mind.

Bernard Gutteridge, who was born in 1916 and fought in the
Burma campaign with Combined Operations, has, in his poetry,
more restricted aims than Henderson, in fact some of his work
might reasonably be called verse-journalism of a very high
order, but within self-imposed limits his poems are generally
more fully achieved than those of the Scot and his best verse has
retained, after almost thirty years, much of its readability. It is
curious that, although Bernard Gutteridge played an active
part in one of the most gruelling and brutal campaigns of the
war, very few of his poems deal directly with what it was like
to fight in the jungle against the Japanese. One that does come
to grips with an incident of battle, *The Enemy Dead*, bears a
superficial resemblance to Keith Douglas's *Vergissmeinicht*:

The dead are always searched.
It's not a man, the blood-soaked
Mess of rice and flesh and bones
Whose pockets you flip open;
And these belongings are only
The counterpart to scattered ball
Or the abandoned rifle.

Yet later the man lives.
His postcard of a light blue
Donkey and sandy minarets
Reveals a man at last.
'Object—the panther mountains!
Two—a tired soldier of Kiku!
Three—my sister the bamboo sigh!'

Then again the man dies.
And only what he has seen
And felt, loved and feared
Stays as a hill, a soldier, a girl:
Are printed in the skeleton
Whose white bones divide and float away
Like nervous birds in the sky.

When compared with *Vergissmeinicht,* the development and resolution of *The Enemy Dead* are oddly evasive of the reality they purport to explore and the final stanza, especially its last two lines, seems to turn away from the stark facts of human mortality to offer a consolatory and inappropriately dainty image.

There is, throughout the war poems collected in *A Traveller's Eye,* a reluctance to contend with the harsher and more savage elements of war and when Gutteridge treats of sexual desire in the soldier exiled to a strange land it is in a flippant way, attractive enough but again conveying the feeling that the reality is being sidestepped.

> Big bummed and bubbed
> The bibis walk down to the Joffre memorial:
> Native policemen white clubbed
> And Catholic priests censorial.
> All the British soldiery there
> Taking it in with a bold stare:
> Black bottoms through chiffon gleaming,
> Sunlight streaming
> And the come-hither air.

The second and last stanza does not, as one might expect, probe deeper into what lies behind that 'bold stare': it is all rather jolly and fundamentally innocent:

> British soldiery gay as a lark
> Wink at each other, all remark
> Black posteriors blandly weaving,
> Sunlight leaving
> All the fun of the dark.

Bernard Gutteridge's wartime poems are, without exception, elegant, observant and intelligent but the poet's studious avoidance of the dramatic which, one suspects, stems from a fear

of the melodramatic, robs them of the intensity which charac-
terises the desert poems of Keith Douglas and the best of Alun
Lewis's poetry from the Far East.

Another poet who served in the same theatre of operations
was R. N. Currey, a South African born in 1907, educated at
Wadham College, Oxford, and a schoolmaster before the war.
His first collection of war poetry, *This Other Planet*, is a sequence
of interrelated poems which chart the transition from civilian to
soldier of an archetypal man of his time and place, a man who,
like the author, is part alien because of his exotic nativity, and
part European or British because of his cultural and historic
roots. Currey uses a variety of forms, loosely sprung rhythm,
free verse, octosyllabic rhyming couplets, sonnets and rhymed
quatrains, but despite this apparent versatility his work is not
distinguished by marked rhythmic vitality or freshness. The
opening section of the sequence, *Outer Seas,* is ponderously
prosaic:

> Air routes now
> Constrict the ball of earth, bring Hawaii
> Almost to picknicking distance; yet we still
> Lean out, as leaves to sun, towards those
> > places
> That keep the flavour of distance. Is exile
> > possible,
> Absolute exile to some triangle between air
> > routes,
> Unshrivelled yet by speed?

And when Currey attempts to convey the actuality of an air raid,
the events and objects are obscured rather than defined by the
proliferation of metaphor:

> The air, the glare,
> Air full of the glare
> Of planes, of rhododendrons;

No patch of shade in which to hide
Except beneath those rhododendrons.

The brilliant sky a rhododendron bush
Turned inside out, a peacock's tail of eyes,
Each arrogant as a peacock, each a sun
Detached from molten skies
Falling as down the barrel of a gun.

Along the road the bomb-bursts, livid bushes
Planted and flowering in an instant;
Flowering among the velvet, glossy-splendid,
Sun-spotted, sheltering rhododendrons.

This is pretty bad writing and, had Currey not done better than
this, he would not have been worthy of mention here, but the
sequence improves considerably as it proceeds and the poet
proves to be at his best when least ambitious and pretentious,
content to embody his perceptions in prescribed metres and
colloquial language, fixing his attention firmly on the object, as
in the three sonnets, the first of which begins 'This is a damned
inhuman sort of war . . .' and the third, ending:

That frame like a picked fish-bone, sprawled
       beneath—
Charred bodies, more like trunks of trees than
       men;
The ammunition began to go up then,
Another and more glittering type of spray;
We could not help them, six men burned to
       death—
I've had their burnt flesh in my lungs all day!

I find his next collection, *Indian Landscape*, less interesting than
This Other Planet because the descriptive poems which make up
the book, while competently executed and occasionally striking
—as in *Bombay Presidency*—are too little influenced by the

circumstances of war and the poet's experience of being a
soldier in a foreign land rather than a camera-toting tourist. Too
many of these poems, concerned as they are with the landscape,
architecture and the religious customs and myths of the country,
might have been written at any time by a sensitive and observant
poet of real but modest talent but they can be called war poems
only insofar as they were written in time of war by a temporary
soldier who would not, in all likelihood, have visited the
country whose features he records except for these circumstances.

R. N. Currey is the author of the British Council pamphlet,
Poets of the 1939–1945 War, and in this essay he refers to F. T.
Prince, mentioning this poet's *Soldiers Bathing* as '. . . perhaps the
most distinguished single poem of the war'. 'Distinguished' is a
question-begging epithet but this poem was almost certainly
more widely praised and discussed during and immediately after
the war than any other piece of verse written at that time and
Currey is echoing an almost unanimously accepted contemporary estimate of Prince's best-known work.

F. T. Prince, who was born in 1912 and—like Currey—a
native of South Africa—was educated at both Oxford and
Princeton Universities. He served with the Intelligence Corps
in the Middle East but of his wartime verse only *Soldiers
Bathing* deals directly with a theme presented by the fact of his
being a soldier, and even here the incident (of watching the men
in his unit enjoying a bathe in the sea) is curiously unreal,
related as it is to paintings by Michelangelo and Pollaiuolo and
to the crucifixion of Jesus Christ. Prince had already, before the
war, shown himself to be a skilful writer whose verses were
resourcefully made if generally derivative in style, almost
everything that he had written evincing a cultivated and fastidious mind, but the transition from a scholarly peacetime
existence to the life of a soldier in time of war seemed scarcely
to affect the kind of poetry he was writing.

Soldiers Bathing is composed in rhymed couplets, the second
line of each pair containing either one or two more metrical feet
than the line with which it rhymes and the verse movement is

slow, reflective and dignified, though the reader might occasionally be disconcerted by unexpected clumsiness of phrasing or
syntax as in the awkward inversion and thumping rhyme in the
last line of the opening paragraph.

> The sea at evening moves across the sand.
> Under a reddening sky I watch the freedom of
> a band
> Of soldiers who belong to me. Stripped bare
> For bathing in the sea, they shout and run in
> the warm air;
> Their flesh worn by the trade of war, revives
> And my mind towards the meaning of it
> strives.

Apart from the technical mismanagement in the last couplet
quoted I find further cause for uneasiness in the tone of 'soldiers
who belong to me'. I take it that no irony is intended here and I
can imagine what the reaction of those soldiers would be if they
had been told that they were the property of the poet and
officer.

In the second paragraph Prince sees the nakedness of the
swimmers as a state symbolising an innocence of which they have
been deprived, at least partially, by their 'trade of war', but
there is something a little soft and sentimental in the language,
something self-conscious in the rhetoric and in the quotation
from *King Lear* that blurs the physical immediacy of the scene.

> . . . . 'Poor bare forked
> animal,'
> Conscious of his desires and needs and flesh
> that rise and fall,
> Stands in the soft air, tasting after toil
> The sweetness of his nakedness: letting the
> sea-waves coil
> Their frothy tongues about his feet, forgets
> His hatred of the war, its terrible pressure that
> begets

A machinery of death and slavery,
Each being a slave and making slaves of
                              others: finds that he
Remembers his old freedom in a game
Mocking himself, and comically mimics fear
                              and shame.

In the next paragraph Prince is reminded of 'Michelangelo's cartoon / Of soldiers bathing . . .' and this memory and his reflection upon it leads to:

Another Florentine, Pollaiuolo,
Painted a naked battle: warriors, straddled,
                              hacked the foe,
Dug their bare toes into the ground and slew
The brother-naked man who lay between their
                              feet and drew
His lips back from his teeth with a grimace.

Then follows a—to me—rather vague meditation on the crucifixion and on the love of God which, in some way that I am not quite able to follow;

            . . . . has driven us to this fury, for
                              so few
Can suffer all the terror of that love:
The terror of that love has set us spinning in
                              this groove
Greased with our blood.

The poem ends with a return from the contemplation of the great abstractions of divine love, terror, and human bestiality to the twentieth-century squaddies who have completed their bathe, but the very last lines are soft with the vague and over-sweet mysticism that I believe to be a fundamental weakness in *Soldiers Bathing*.

In his other poems written during the war there is either no reference at all to external events or, where the war is referred to, it provides only a remote backdrop against which the more crucial conflicts are enacted, that is to say the conflicts between body and soul, the co-existent brutality and spirituality in man's nature, the struggle to reconcile human with divine love, Eros with Agape, and not only do the stink and violence of a world in arms make little or no real impact upon Prince's verse, the presence of personal human love is etiolated by a mannered intellectualisation of the way it operates. The seventeenth-century metaphysical poets have obviously exercised a strong influence over Prince's poetics. Take these lines from *The Book*:

> You are periphery;
> And we would be the centre, if we could
> But break your circle, or could be
> Without you, inconceivably
> Ourselves our multitude and solitude.
> You would be nothing then,
> As now all other things and men
> Are turned to nothing at a touch
> Of hand or lip; again,
> We'd seek the soul, and having passed
> Through you and through ourselves, at last
> Find the dark kingdom that denies that such
> As selves, and thoughts and bodies, matter
>   much.

This is wonderfully adroit pastiche but, as a love poem written in the Second World War, I find it almost laughably out of touch with its time and circumstance and, even more so than *Soldiers Bathing*, it seems remarkable for its insulation from the hard facts of what was actually happening to millions of people, collectively and individually, all over the world.

Where F. T. Prince largely evades the temporal and local realities of war by self-immersion in metaphysics explored behind the cold shield of a classical style, Jocelyn Brooke, who saw service with the Royal Army Medical Corps in North

Africa and Italy, appears to seek, if not a refuge, at least some consolation and reassurance by adopting an uncompromisingly romantic stance. He shows nothing like the intelligence and formal dexterity of Prince and there are few poems in his collection, *December Spring*, which are not encumbered by phrases and images which are familiar stock properties from the late Victorian and lesser Georgian poets—'rain-wet garden', 'darkling meadow', 'kisses stolen in the drenched wood', 'golden and remembered days', 'sad autumnal days', and so on. From these samples alone you might easily guess that Brooke's prevailing tone is one of quiet melancholy and nostalgic retrospection and most of the war poems do indeed reflect these moods, but occasionally, and most clearly in a poem called *April—Italy 1944,* a note emerges which is extremely rare in the English poetry of the Second World War yet one which reveals a response to service life which to some degree was very widely felt, a sense almost of euphoria, certainly of contentment, that came from living at a level of simplicity virtually impossible to discover in any other situation, a mode of existence where basic physical needs were all catered for, the complexities of adult civilian life removed and the world felt and observed with something very like the freshness of a child's perception. It is true that these moments occurred less frequently and perhaps less purely than the retrospection of middle-aged ex-servicemen is sometimes likely to claim, but occur they did, and Brooke is one of the very few serious poets to record such an experience at the time of its happening. The poem begins:

Now in these April evenings
With soft and petalled airs,
And the quick burst of thunder
And sudden April rain
And the guns behind the mountains
Answering the thunder—
Now in this insidious
And soft green twilight,
The Spring resumes again
Its sly, oblique offensive,
Like the foreseen relapse

Of a recurrent fever:
Disturbing the designed
And static winter living
With the wild narcissus
And limbs bared to sunlight,
The soldier in shirt-sleeve order
And blossoming almond . . . .

There follows a lyrical celebration of the beauties of the Spring landscape and flowers and Brooke nicely captures the ambivalent sense of well-being that is, at the same time, elusively sad, yet with a melancholy that is at least partly pleasurable. The poem ends with:

A swaddie alakefak
In a cushy unit, sweating
On a home-posting, but glad
Of this kind and smiling country
And the sexual flowers,
The men like trees walking
In the haunted sunset hours,
And the friendly houses under
The olive-terraced hill,
With the wine and easy talking
In the darkening, still
Evenings haunted by thunder.

Brooke writes more conventionally of the uniformed civilian's sense of loss and alienation in poems like *California* and *Three Barrows Down* where Edward Thomas would seem to be his model, though he lacks the earlier poet's brooding power and vision. Some of his less ambitious but arguably more successful lyrics can still be read with enjoyment, poems like *Soldier's Song* in which the barrack-room vernacular is used to supply an agreeably jaunty music.

O Death be kind to the swaddie,
The man with a load of bull—

Be kind to the muscled body,
  Thumbs-up and belly-full.

Browned-off with the bints and boozing,
  Sweating on news from home,
Bomb-happy and scared of losing
  This tent of flesh and bone . . . .

If, in their different ways, F. T. Prince and Jocelyn Brooke sought in their poetry to evade direct confrontation with those aspects of the war which were so terrible that, both as artists and as men, they might well have been overwhelmed, the one as a neo-metaphysical and the other as a romantic lyricist, Gavin Ewart's approach to the material supplied by the Second World War was essentially that of the satirist, employing the weapon of a defensive irony against the crudities, boredom, absurdities, austerities and horrors of the situation.

Officers' Mess, which was first published in *Horizon* in 1942, is a fairly blunt but nevertheless effective attack on the boozy boastfulness, stupidity, prejudice and immaturity that was so often encountered among officers in all branches of the services.

It's going to be a thick night tonight (and the
        night before was a thick one);
I've just seen the Padre disappearing into 'The
        Cock and Bull' for a quick one.
I don't mind telling you this, old boy, we got
        the Major drinking—
You probably know the amount of gin he's in
        the habit of sinking—
And then that new M.O. came in, the Jewish
        one, awful fellow,
And his wife, a nice little bit of stuff, dressed
        in a flaming yellow.
Looked a pretty warmish piece, old boy—no
        have this one with me—
They were both so blind (and so was the
        Major) that they could hardly see.

And so it goes on, the emphatic rhythm and thumping rhymes
adding a kind of jovial desperation to the poet's sense of isolation and his disgust. *Oxford Leave* has the same cantering energy
but the sharpness of the satire is tempered by an underlying
geniality. A later poem, *When A Beau Goes In,* though more
restrained in tone, is sharper in its attack on the heartlessness
that lay behind the facile attitudes and jargon of journalists and
Blimps.

> When a Beau goes in,
> Into the drink,
> It makes you think,
> Because, you see, they always sink
> But nobody says 'Poor lad'
> Or goes about looking sad
> Because, you see, it's war,
> It's the unalterable law.
>
> Although it's perfectly certain
> The pilot's gone for a Burton
> And the observer too
> It's nothing to do with you
> And if they both should go
> To a land where falls no rain nor hail nor
> driven snow—
> Here, there or anywhere,
> Do you suppose *they* care?
>
> You shouldn't cry
> Or say a prayer or sigh.
> In the cold sea, in the dark,
> It isn't a lark
> But it isn't Original Sin—
> It's just a Beau going in.

The sonnet beginning 'The point where beauty and intelligence meet . . .' is a well-turned love poem, conventional
enough until the last line when Ewart's defensive irony in the
phrase 'fear of the young' modifies what has gone before.

And I before the happy, tough battalions
Engulf me or the frozen seas of Norway,
Have still my dreams of cities and of
                                    dalliance,
But most of you as standing in a doorway,
Who might, though I so dissipate my life,
Be mistress or, fear of the young, a wife.

For Whom the Bell Tolls is a stylish and witty reflection on the
uncertainty of survival in time of war and *Cigarette For the
Bambino*, a less successful (partly because he uses free verse in
which he is noticeably less at home than in traditional metres)
anti-clerical squib which for once slips over into cliché attitudes
and sentimentality, but in at least one poem he puts aside his
satirical armoury and writes a simple and moving sonnet on
War Dead:

With grey arm twisted over a green face
The dust of passing trucks swirls over him,
Lying by the roadside in his proper place,
For he has crossed the ultimate far rim
That hides from us the valley of the dead.
He lies like used equipment thrown aside,
Of which our swift advance can take no heed,
Roses, triumphal cars—but this one died.

Once war memorials, pitiful attempt
In some vague way regretfully to atone
For those lost futures that the dead had
                                    dreamt,
Covered the land with their lamenting stone—
But in our hearts we bear a heavier load:
The bodies of the dead beside the road.

Another poet who, like Ewart, adopted an anti-heroic and
satirical approach to the experience of soldiering was Norman
Cameron, but there are differences in tone and strategy in the

work of these poets. Cameron, who was born in 1905 and died in 1953, was a friend and I think it would not be an exaggeration to say, a disciple of Robert Graves whose voice he sometimes echoes with almost uncanny verisimilitude, commanding a language that is both simple and fluent, formal and precise yet never quite the speech of his time, a kind of private vernacular which, while carrying echoes of the speech and cadences of a more gracious past, retain, if not a note of modernity, then one of curious timelessness, though in the few poems he wrote directly from his experience of the war he chose to write in a less idiosyncratic, more neutral style. *Black Takes White* is a cool satirical piece, a comment on war's absurdity, and it embodies, without either approval or disapproval, an attitude of racial prejudice that was pervasive in all ranks of the British Forces during the Second World War. This prejudice was generally expressed in jocular, even quite affectionate terms, but the fact remains that it was deep-rooted and ubiquitous and behind it lay an unquestioning assumption of national superiority that— in its flippant or understated way—was perilously close to the murderous racialism of the Nazis.

Black Takes White—the title's suggestion of a game of draughts or checkers points to the position the whole poem adopts— tells in loosely rhymed couplets the story of how a German unit was established in an almost impregnable position in the Appenines and they were faced by an American force, neither side being able to take the initiative. The Americans had Negroes in their ranks and the Germans were supported by their allies, the Italians.

> The only major movement in those quarters
> Was a dense, two-way traffic of deserters.

In the next paragraph Cameron describes what happens when a party of Negro deserters from the American lines meets 'a like-minded Eyetie', each group insisting that they should be the captives of the other. The argument is resolved by the fact that the Italian party is led by an officer:

The Eyeties held the trump, the winning
                                        factor:
Their lot was led by an ufficiale;
What *he* said, went. 'The tale's a tribute, really,
To both sides' rather narrow sense of duty.'
Back marched the Negroes with their
                                unsought booty.

When the two parties return to the American sector the Negroes
are treated as heroes:

Nobody paused to bother with such trifles
As where the captors had mislaid their rifles.
Quickly those fed-up and embarrassed Negroes
Were praised, promoted, given gongs as
                                heroes,
And photographs of their victorious battle
Were published from Long Island to Seattle.

The poem is well-made, the off-hand style, the rhythmic
shifts and off-rhymes combine to give flavour and sharpness to
the irony and the satire seems to look forward to the much later
and, of course, more savage surrealistic attacks on the futility of
war such as *Catch 22* and the film M.A.S.H.

Another war poem by Cameron is set in North Africa and
while it is very similar in form, in its vocabulary and rhythms
which never move far from their sources in common speech, its
content and feeling are entirely different. *Green, Green is El
Aghir* takes as its theme the fact that the physical hardships
endured by the serviceman gave to his moments of respite and
ease a value that they would not in time of peace have possessed:
to relieve thirst with plain water could become a sensation close
to ecstasy after a long journey by Army truck in the dust and
heat of the African sun.

It was eighty more kilometres
Until round a corner we heard a splashing of
                                waters,

And there, in a green, dark street, was a
                fountain with two faces
Discharging both ways, from full-throated
                faucets
Into basins, thence into troughs and thence
                into brooks.
Our Negro corporal driver slammed his
                brakes,
And we yelped and leapt from the truck and
                went at the double
To fill our bidons and bottles and drink and
                dabble.

Green, Green is El Aghir is that rare thing, a poem dealing with an incident of war which is celebratory, though naturally in a subdued and slightly ironic way. It differs sharply from Jocelyn Brooke's affirmative *April—Italy 1944* for, where Brooke's tone is romantic and his rhythms gently predictable, Cameron corrects any slant towards an oversoft music with his variety of pace and use of pararhyme.

Keith Douglas, Alun Lewis, and Sidney Keyes, the three outstanding soldier-poets of the Second World War, all lost their lives in the conflict and it is sad, tantalising and finally purposeless to speculate on how each would have developed had he survived. But at least all of these poets in their different ways and to varying degrees achieved a measure of artistic fulfilment and, in the case of Douglas, left behind a body of work which I am sure must find a secure place in the literature of our time.

In *Eight Oxford Poets,* edited by Michael Meyer and Sidney Keyes and published during 1941—it contained work by Keith Douglas as well as by Keyes and his friend, John Heath-Stubbs —appeared four poems by a young undergraduate at Queen's College, Drummond Allison who was born in 1921. Allison joined the East Surrey Regiment and was killed in Italy in 1943. He published posthumously a single collection of poems, *The*

Yellow Night, but although he was a young man of unquestion-
able talent, intelligence and imaginative vigour and much of
what he wrote was both interesting and enjoyable, there is
scarcely a poem which convinces you that it is a completely
realised work of art.

His early poems are characteristic of the kind of undergraduate writing that comes from bright but immature minds
which have recently encountered a wide range of new and
exciting ideas, browsed copiously in libraries but been unable
fully to assimilate and relate to the ordinary business of living
the thrilling and often shadowy notions that jostle and clamour
in the imagination. Allison wrote a number of heavily alliterated
verses, influenced either by Old English models or—as seems
more likely—by the early Auden who, with far greater cunning,
had adapted some of the techniques and cadances of *Beowulf* and
The Exeter Book for his own purposes in such works as *Paid on
Both Sides* and *The Orators.* Allison's apprentice poems were
furnished with imagery drawn from a preoccupation with
Arthurian legend but these images are never quite successfully
married to his immediate concerns as a young man from the
privileged middle classes who recognises the justice of the
Marxist case but cannot cast away his loyalty, nurtured by
breeding, education and filial affection, to his own family and
class, a young man, too, about to be involved as a soldier in the
enormous adventure of the Second World War.

The Yellow Night shows a gradual movement away from
Allison's ambitious but muddled attempts at myth-making and
some adolescent nose-thumbing at death, through some sharp
and witty social comment in *We Shall Have Company* and *From
Wales Where Whistling Miners,* towards a verse which more
modestly and with correspondingly greater success attempts to
define and fix his private response to events against the great
backcloth of wartime England. Yorktown *Gate Guard* is a love
poem—or, rather, an anti-love poem—which draws its imagery
from details of the military life and the menaces of the battlefields and beleagured towns.

> Another August, far too shy to shout,
> I flushed and stood aside and let you out;

But now, my bearskin doffed and buttons dull,
A point shall threaten your quiet skin and
                                        skull.

Henceforth your last year's permit won't avail
And I'll suspect there's gas in every gale:
The bombed old buildings of my heart still
                                        hide
A Certain Thing whose worth we can't
                                        confide.

So you'd best gather up your floral gown
For good and cadge a lift to London Town
Whither with its impatience and its power
These lonely lorries lumber every hour.

Written from Plymouth is an accurate description of bleak
wartime England and the last poem in the book, *The Cold
Thoughts*, is probably his most fully realised work where style
and subject matter are more happily blended than is usual
elsewhere in this collection and something approaching an
individual voice can be discerned.

              . . . . But now the Baker Man
Warms up the engine of his different van
—Now round and numbered is the noisy bread
Of war he must distribute—and in vain
Warns us of what we were: the sticks who ran,
The flying child, the optimistic dead . . . .

The end of the poem is less controlled than the beginning but
one feels poignantly that this lack of coherence is a guarantee of
the emotional force that has broken the ordered pattern, that
Allison is struggling to give expression to fears that are almost
impossible to identify:

. . . . The truthful tapes are
running
Across the minefields of my fear, and I
Can trace and follow them tonight. Though by
Fast flare and Verey light I see the tombs
Of what my cold thoughts killed or what my
darling
Had put to death by tolerance, I say:
'Synchronise watches, we are going dancing,
are advancing,
Spite of the blinded windows and the jaundice
of the Thames.'

There were, as I remarked earlier, many more than those
whose work I have here discussed who served in the United
Kingdom's armed forces during the Second World War and
wrote verses that proceeded from that experience, but to list
them would be uninstructive. What might be more worth
commenting on is the fact that, of all the poets of minor or
major achievement whose writings we have looked at here,
there is not one who served with the Royal Air Force. This does
not mean that there was no verse written or published by
airmen, but simply that there was little of intrinsic literary value.
There were various reasons why this should have been so.

By far the largest percentage of conscripted men was drafted
into one or other branch of the Army, and R.A.F. personnel,
especially members of air crews, contained large numbers of
volunteers. The type of young man who was attracted to flying
tended to be more interested in machines than in the arts and,
while of course it would be quite wrong to assume that there
was a stereotyped young airman, inarticulate, extrovert and not
overbright, there were nevertheless plenty of such 'Flying-
Officer Kytes' in the service and these would be more likely to
spend their leisure time sinking beer in the mess or local pub
than in the solitary reading or writing of poetry. Even those
members of air crew who possessed the temperament and
ability to write verse would probably find it harder than the
average soldier or sailor to find the spare time and relief from
tension needed for reflection and composition, for most men in

the Army and Navy knew more or less prolonged periods when there was little to do beyond performing the mechanical duties of guards, watches, parades and the like. Not only were the air crews continually in action or undergoing the stress of standing-by prepared for take-off, the actual business of flying could be intensely absorbing, exciting and to some pilots it was an end in itself, a quasi-mystical experience which would elude the net of language. Finally, it is tragically true that, of the young flying men who did write and publish verses, few lived long enough to mature as artists.

Timothy Corsellis, who published a number of very romantic poems in wartime journals and anthologies, was killed at the age of twenty. It is impossible to say whether or not he would have developed into a poet of any stature, for the work he left behind is not really much different from the better sixth-form verse one sees in school magazines, though of course it has acquired an extra-literary poignancy from the circumstances of its author's life and death. Brian Allwood, who was killed in Italy at the age of twenty-four, wrote with more craft and control than Corsellis and he possessed a modest but genuine talent which understood its own limitations, but of Keith Foottit, T. R. Hodgson, David Raikes, Nigel Weir and James Farrar, all of whom lost their lives in action, only the last named showed signs of real promise. So, if what I have said is accepted, it is not surprising that the only R.A.F. verse that might properly claim to be judged by professional standards was written, not by operational airmen, but by men with ground jobs of one kind or another.

John Pudney's facile verses were popular during the war but their shallow sentimentality would be unlikely to find admirers now. Herbert Corby wrote some neat and unpretentious poems which show clear affinities with the Georgians: at his worst he aped Rupert Brooke:

> Whenever hearts have song and minds have
> peace
> or in your eyes the prides of banners burn,
> think of these who dreamed and loved as you,
> and gave their laughter, gave their sun and
> snow,

their English grave blessed by their native dew
that you would live . . . .

but when he focused his attention on the immediate facts and
objects of R.A.F. life he could write sharply and pleasingly as in
this little poem, *Reprisal*:

They worked all night with cardboard and
                    with wood
to make those dummy planes to hoodwink
                    the foe,
and in the chilly morning solitude
wheeled out the dummies to places they
                    should go
on the dispersal fields, and went away;
the hours passed uneventfully, and even
no reconnaissance planes were overhead that
                    day.
They evacuated in the twilight, just after
                    seven,
and when they'd gone the Germans flew
                    above the drome
and by each plane they dropped a wooden
                    bomb.

John Bayliss, another air force poet, produced some wartime
verse which to my mind has been unjustly ignored by many
recent anthologists and literary historians of the period, though
it is true that some of his poems are so generalised that they
might have been written by a member of any of the forces or
indeed by a civilian. *Home Thoughts From Abroad,* for example,
could more plausibly refer to the First World War than the
Second with its references to '. . . bayonet and blood / Stamped
in the mud among fallen leaves', '. . . scarecrows on the barbed
wire' and not a single mention of aerial combat, but when he
takes a subject from the situation at hand he can write movingly,
as he does in his irregular sonnet, *Reported Missing*:

With broken wing they limped across the sky
caught in late sunlight, with their gunner dead,
one engine gone,—the type was out-of-date,—
blood on the fuselage turning brown from red:

knew it was finished, looking at the sea
which shone back patterns in kaleidoscope
knew that their shadow would meet them by
                                    the way,
close and catch at them, drown their single
                              hope:

sat in this tattered scarecrow of the sky
hearing it cough, the great plane catching
now the first dark clouds upon her wing-
                              base,—
patching the great tear in evening mockery.

So two men waited, saw the third dead face,
and wondered when the wind would let them
                              die.

The lesser but genuine poets of the Second World War—
writers such as Bayliss, Ewart, Henderson and Gutteridge, to
name a few—were certainly as plentiful as those of the Great
War, and I believe that the standard of their work was at least as
high as that of the war poets of their fathers' generation and, as
with the more important talents, their range was wider. The
poetry of the First World War fell broadly into four categories:
the poetry of celebration which paid tribute to the courage and
fortitude of the fighting men or praised the values of comradeship, loyalty and honour that flourished in the trenches;
descriptive verse which attempted to re-create and preserve the
nightmare geography of the battlefields for future generations to
contemplate with pity and horror; elegiac poetry of grief for the
dead and, finally, the literature of protest and indignation
which included, of course, satire.
    The poetry of the Second World War dealt with all of these
themes but it also—in Fuller and Lewis, for example—explored

the political problems and analogues presented by the war, and, in Keith Douglas, Henry Reed and others, is to be found a metaphysical subtlety and richness that is absent from a great deal of the poetry of 1914–18. I am not maintaining that the poetry of the Second World War is 'better' than that of the previous World War, only that it should be taken as seriously, and I hope that I have done something towards convincing those readers who believed that the 1939–45 hostilities failed to produce any poetry of quality that they have been mistaken and that, just as the First World War poetry enables us to know imaginatively the horror and glory of those terrible events, to recapture the sense of what it was really like, so the poetry of the Second War conveys the true feeling of those desolate and desperate days with an urgency and sense of truth that no other means of recording could emulate.

American Poets of the
Second World War

On December 4, 1941, the Japanese attacked Pearl Harbour and struck simultaneous blows on the Philippines and Malaya and, on the following day, the United States declared war on the aggressors. Three days later Germany and Italy joined Japan in war against the United States and the Americans were plunged into the maelstrom in which for almost two years the British and Commonwealth forces had been struggling, virtually alone, against the Axis Forces. The American poets who either volunteered for, or were drafted into one or other of the armed services found themselves, as writers, in a quite different situation from that which their British counterparts had known in 1939, for, in the literature of the United States there was no substantial tradition of poetry from the trenches, nor had the British poets of the 1914–1918 war exercised any significant influence on American writing between the wars.

The United States forces in the First World War did not effectively enter the arena until well into 1918, six months before the armistice and, although a handful of poets, among them E. E. Cummings and John Peale Bishop, did write a few poems directly inspired by their experiences on active service, these works were exiguous and not essentially different from the other writings of the authors concerned. In other words there was not a genre of 'war poetry', nothing to compare with the work of Sassoon, Sorley, Owen, Blunden and Rosenberg which, by 1939, had become part of the literary consciousness of all young British poets, presenting a starting-point from which to continue and develop or against which to react and seek new modes of expression appropriate to the altered subjective and objective conditions of the second Great War. Some of the most promising of the young American poets writing at the time of Pearl Harbour who were yet to reach creative maturity—that is to say poets of a suitable age for military service such as Randall Jarrell, Karl Shapiro, Howard Nemerov and Richard Wilbur— were influenced strongly by the New Criticism's conservatism with its emphasis on formal orthodoxy, good manners, elegance and wit, and they aimed at producing a poetry that was primarily metaphysical and aesthetic rather than concerned with exploring an historical reality for the purpose of discovering psychological or moral truths. They had not suffered, as their British coevals had, the vicarious experience of four years of monstrous suffering and waste in the trenches of Flanders—or, to put it another way, the First World War had not become for them a powerful tragic myth but was, rather, a national triumph, one episode in a saga of success—nor had they ever known enemy attacks on their own cities, as had Britain in both wars, with the Zeppelin raids on London in the First and, of course, the savage holocausts of the Blitz in the Second. It is noticeable that some of the best American poetry of the Second World War was written after the poets had returned to civilian life. Howard Nemerov, Louis Simpson and Anthony Hecht all wrote good poems whose roots lay in their experience of war, but these were retrospective works and it seems that the nature of the poets' training and talents, the entire approach to their craft, required a distancing from events before they were able to transmute the raw material provided by their wartime lives into the permanence of art.

There were a few exceptions to these generalizations, notably Randall Jarrell and Karl Shapiro, both of whom were published and highly regarded during or immediately after the war, but there is one American author who, to my mind, wrote some of the most extraordinary war poetry to come from either side of the Atlantic in the Second World War and this poet has, even now, gained little more than a coterie reputation in the United

States and is almost unknown in Britain. I refer to Lincoln Kirstein who, before the war, as a Harvard undergraduate, founded and edited the remarkable literary magazine, *Hound & Horn* and, after serving as a private soldier in various theatres of war, returned to peacetime civilian life to become famous as an impresario and General Director of the New York City Ballet. His collection of war poems, *Rhymes and More Rhymes of a P.F.C*, could lay serious claim to being the most original volume to be inspired by the Second World War.

Rhymes of a P.F.C. is a substantial book, containing eighty-five poems which are divided into five main sections—*Stateside*, *U.K.*, *France*, *Germany*, and *Peace*, with an opening trio of poems under the general heading, *World War I*, and a *Postscript* of four pieces. The originality of Kirstein's collection does not reside in formal experimentation in the usual sense of the term; on the contrary, every poem in the book is written to a strict pattern of orthodox metre and rhyme, collectively suggesting a variety of mainly British models, a most unlikely group which would include Thomas Hardy, W. S. Gilbert, Rudyard Kipling, A. E. Housman, John Betjeman, and—unless I am much mistaken—Gerard Manley Hopkins; these curiously unfashionable and—one would have thought—unserviceable influences are drawn together to weave a style which, despite the echoes, is strangely and completely his own, and—paradoxically in view of the Englishness of his exemplars—speaks with an unequivocally American voice.

An inattentive reader might be deceived by the superficial conventionality of the forms employed, the regularity of metrical patterns, the invariable use of rhyme, the lightness of touch, the wit and the frequent use of phonetic spelling, into regarding Kirstein's work as mere light verse. It is not light verse, but poetry of some depth and feeling which explores aspects of war and the military life at various levels which were of perennial interest to those who were involved in the situation, aspects, however, which are rarely, if ever, dealt with by other war poets though they will be more familiar to readers of the best prose fiction of the Second World War. He writes of homosexual relationships in service life, both satirically and more tenderly; he is much concerned with the injustices and absurdities of the hierarchical caste system on which military discipline and good order is founded, with racial conflict between black and white serving in the same army against a common enemy, the importance of the role played by whores in a soldier's life, with the black market and, perhaps most perceptively, with physical fear and its sexual connotations and the tragi-comic predicament of the sensitive, fastidious, timid—perhaps effeminate—man in the brutal, dangerous and deadening environment of military life.

Louis Simpson, whose retrospective war poems are among the best by American ex-service writers, has written about his own work dealing with war:[32]

> What, in these poems, was I trying to do that had not already been done? I did not wish to protest against war. Any true description of modern warfare is a protest, but many have written against war with satire or indignation, and it still goes on. My object was to remember. I wished to show the war exactly, as though I were painting a landscape or a face. I wanted people to find in my poems the truth of what it had been like to be an American infantry soldier. Now I see that I was writing a memorial of those years, for the me I had known, who were silent. I was trying to write poems that I would not be ashamed to have them read—poems that would be, in their laconic and simple manner, tolerable to men who had seen a good deal of combat and had no illusions.

But Simpson's poems of war, excellent though they are, direct, honest and carefully made, would not, I feel, command the interest and affections of an ordinary non-literary—perhaps scarcely literate—soldier, because their quality—and this is not to belittle them in any way—owes as much to a sophisticated literary tradition as to the experiences with which they deal, a tradition which is essentially aristocratic and metaphysical. 'Laconic and simple' these poems may be to the educated, practised reader of modern verse, but I doubt if many working-class enlisted men would find them so. Kirstein's achievement is to produce poems many of which, if read to a heterogenous audience of soldiers, from buck private to General, would, I am sure, provide instant and deep pleasure to everyone present; he has created a genuinely popular art but his work not only stands up to examination on the page, it discloses subtleties which demand the most serious critical appraisal.

The first poem in *Rhymes of a P.F.C.* does not deal directly with war but it does sound a thematic chord which is to be repeated with variations through the book: this theme is a deep concern with the contradictions and paradoxes that abound in manifestations of human fear and courage and with the predicament of the timid man compelled to adopt a martial role and face appalling demands which he is ill-equipped to meet. The poem, *Fall In*, whose title, with prophetic irony, anticipates the military command, is like all the work collected in *Rhymes of a P.F.C.* built upon a firm narrative base: a young boy, the narrator, is taken by his uncle to '. . . the big boys' club, / Where they swam nude, drank beer, shared secrecy.' The child, who evidently cannot swim, is terrified when he realises that his roughneck uncle is going to force him into the swimming pool, so, in desperation, he throws himself into the water and pretends to drown, and it is the adult who is then the frightened one:

> He tugged me out with terror, even awe.
>   I felt my fright infect his grizzled chest;
> Palpating this drowned rat to retch and drain,
>   He knew I knew who'd flunked his foolish test.

> Thus one bears fear in action, guilt in pride.
>   I was his sister's son, yet still no male.
> The spineless kin he'd vowed to make a man
>   Confounded polity and saw him fail.

> The rage of armies is the shame of boys;
>   A hero's panic or a coward's whim
> Is triggered by nerve or nervousness.
>   We wish to sink. We do not choose to swim.

The second poem, *World War I*, is a childhood memory of the

impact made by the Great War on the poet's German-Jewish
family in the United States, and it recounts the way in which the
young Kirstein learnt more about the real issues of war and of
life from Earl O'Toole, a mulatto janitor, than he had from
parents or teachers:

> Can I ever
> repay
> Him for his grand advisements? He discovers
> a practical way.
>
> In wars the rich are warm enough, the poor
> frequently cold.
> Anthracite or bituminous fuel may not be
> bought or sold,
> Yet with a magic ticket got from he won't
> say where
> They hand me chunky bags of coal simply
> for standing there,
>
> In a queue of wives in shawls with kids,
> gath'ring before the light,
> Shuffling through steel-shovel forenoon deep
> into slip-ice night.

Like the third prefatory poem, *ABC*, which looks back at the
period immediately following the 1914–1918 conflict, and
describes the narrator's fascination with a scarred and shell-
shocked veteran who wanders the nocturnal streets of the poet's
hometown, *World War I* adumbrates many of the preoccupations of the works which form the substance of the collection
and it communicates the sense of the childhood and youth of a
whole generation being haunted by a war that is over and by a
precognitive awareness that all present experience is a preparation for the war to come, and in this Kirstein is closer in spirit to
the work of British Second World War poets than to any other
American whose work I know. But only in this. The speech
rhythms, the witty and vigorous employment of invective and

profanity, the muscularity and sheer energy of the writing are as American as the prose of John Horne Burns, James Jones, Norman Mailer and Joseph Heller yet, since Kirstein is writing poetry, and poetry of a high order, he is able to strike resonances, suggest ambiguities and pack layers of other possible meanings beneath his anecdotal surfaces that are beyond the scope of the novelists.

Basic Training, the first poem in the *Stateside* section, picks up from *Fall In* the situation of the mild and gentle human being forced by the exigencies of war to become an efficient machine of destruction, the 'sissy' as killer. A sardonic description is given of some of the absurdities of military training, the never quite convincing simulation of battle conditions during an exercise, and then the poet, in his ten-minute break from his senseless exertions remembers a childhood friend, Dick Hales:

> His dad, a drunk, tossed him his cavalry
> saber; quit home for worse.
> Dick, a sissy of course,
> Tacked the sword to his wall, whimpered for
> Mummy to come and be kissed;
> Never won games nor a girl; to Canada
> crossed to enlist
> In their Royal Air Force.
>
> Yesterday, in some clippings from home I
> chanced to have read
> Dick Hales is dead.
> Slid his flakkèd plane sidewise low over
> Sussex to spare a girls' school;
> No trick for coward or fool.
> He had the presence of heart or head to make
> his enormous bet.
> Now is he hero, haloed and holy. His mummy
> can get
> Used to life's being cruel.
>
> Dick: what is left of you now, with my civil
> war please coincide.

> Kidding aside,
> Accept sprig of apple or plum which pitiless
> > April has brought,
> The meager tribute I've got;
> First to fall among men I have known, always
> > sure to get hit—
> Or, after the fact, seems so—your crash links
> > history a bit:
> Minié ball, flak, grapeshot.

Kirstein, cultured middle-class intellectual serving in the ranks, gifted with the artist's clear objective eye, is able to view the preposterous, unbridgeable gap between enlisted man and commissioned officer with clarity and he examines his representative types with precision yet with an empathy that holds back indignation from the excesses of rage and hatred. In a later poem, *Rank,* from the *France* section, he tells a bitter tale based on a consequence of the military caste system. The opening stanza states his theme:

> Differences between rich and poor, king and queen,
> Cat and dog, hot and cold, day and night, now
> > and then,
> Are less clearly distinct than all those between
> Officers and us: enlisted men.

The narrator and his friend, Jack, are stationed in a small French town and they have discovered a pleasant café kept by an amiable patron, Jean-Pierre and his attractive, much-loved wife, Marie-Louise. The two enlisted men go there to drink moderately, practise their French and play chess with the local farmers. One night a drunken officer invades their retreat and demands whisky from Jean-Pierre who politely explains that his bar does not sell spirits at all, only beer and wine. The officer, a Captain Stearnes, accepts with very bad grace a glass of beer, but he is unappeased and he turns on the two soldiers who are

sitting with their loaded rifles at their side in accordance with
the rule that they must not go anywhere unarmed in a combat
zone. The drunken captain seizes one of the weapons and
announces that he is going to demonstrate his marksmanship by
cracking the porcelain stove which warms the premises. He fires
wildly, unbalanced by booze and the vigorous kick of the
rifle, misses the stove completely and the bullet pierces the
ceiling and kills Marie-Louise who is sleeping in her bedroom
above the bar. And this is the outcome of his deed:

> Formal enquiry subsequent to this shootin'
> Had truth and justice separately demanded.
> Was Stearnes found guilty? You are darned
> tootin':
> Fined, demoted. More: reprimanded.
>
> The charge was not murder, mayhem,
> mischief malicious,
> Yet something worse, and this they brought
> out time and again;
> Clearly criminal and caddishly vicious
> Was his: Drinking With Enlisted Men.
>
> I'm serious. It's what the Judge Advocate said:
> Strick maintenance of rank or our system is sunk.
> Stearnes saluted. Jean-Pierre wept his dead.
> Jack and I got see-double drunk.

The laconic style, the compression and restraint with which the
story is told, increases the sickening force of its message and
causes it to ring with veracity like a sound coin on a bar.

In another short-story poem, *Interpreter*, the criticism of the
officer by his subordinate is justifiably less acrimonious, suggested rather than stated explicitly, and the enlisted man and his
superior are, by implication, identified by the common factor of
sexual susceptibility. A French girl, suspected of collaboration,

is interrogated by an officer with the aid of his interpreter who
is the narrator of the poem. The captain wants to know if the
girl 'was intimate' with the man she is accused of assisting in his
activities to the disadvantage of the allied cause, but the girl,
with real or assumed ingenuousness, and certainly aware of her
sexual attraction for her inquisitors, replies

> 'Why, yes. He's sweet. I like him well.
>   And what is wrong with that?'
> Stretches, yawns, purrs, spreads herself
>   To curl, a svelte house-cat.

Finally the officer abandons his questioning and he and the
interpreter leave her apartment:

> My captain never will confide
>   In this enlisted dough;
> Aside from rude conjecture I
>   May never really know
> What here's involved; what these kids did,
>   Who caught more than a kiss
> Though on some profounder plane
>   There's nothing much to miss.
> Six tall flights up, the pretty puss
>   Leans at her window pane,
> Idly wondering which of us
>   Will scale her stairs again.

Certainly, one feels, the captain, or both of them at different
times, will return on an unofficial errand, for whatever their
differences in rank, education (it is the enlisted man who speaks
French, not the officer), and temperament they are both equally
responsive to the magnetism of her sex.

Nowhere else in poetry have I read such frank and penetrating
examinations of that special sexuality fostered by the conditions
of military life, the licence extended by the imminence of

violent death and the disturbing relationship between intense physical fear and erotic desire, as in the work of Kirstein. The savage and witty poem, *Load*, is brutally exact about terror under fire seeking relief in the diversion of masturbation. Here is the work in its entirety:

> Our dirty dreams in ragged sleep:
>   Kick off that blanket, creak that cot,
> And all our billet, ankle-deep
>   In dry-lipped dozing, waits the shot.
> Upon some secret siding trained
>   Forty miles over the Moselle
> Nestles a long-range railroad gun
>   Which slings a two-ton super shell.
> It splits some slumber, rips a roof,
>   Priming our chest-pumps overtime;
> Set to sweat out this noisy night
>   We mark the hours' quartered chime.
>
> I am a tube, dry at both vents,
>   My molars ground, my sphincters tight,
> But damp in oxter, palm, and crotch,
>   A hose for cowardice or fright.
> I am a stack of plastic tubes,
>   Liquids and solids to transform;
> Bundled in armies, my moist friends
>   Frame our vast sieve to strain the storm.
> One supple pipe from lip to prick,
>   One coiled long loop from mouth to ass,
> A modest million drippings drain
>   Letting each pissy droplet pass.
>
> These thin-spray every fluent fear,
>   Greasing its shudder, gag, and shock.
> Wow! Here it comes! Just feel this floor
>   Rise to the blast, bend, crack, and rock.
> Well aimed from forty miles away
>   Are steel-turned tubes the Jerries use,
> But the most harm their banging does
>   Is stiffen us to self-abuse.

Waiting the next note from their gun,
  A hot hand strokes an aching hard.
Nervousness exceeding fun
  Jacks a poor peter to its yard.

All eyes and ears on fire, in dark;
  Livid the iced, unspoken noise,
Threatening to madden, stunt the growth
  Of me and my lot of naughty boys.
Kraut cannon crouches, skins it back.
  Self-murder's tool is terror's goad.
It crashes about three blocks off.
  Its big load splashes my small load.

Another poem, *Snatch,* describes the visit of some G.I.s to a French brothel and this work is given a cutting edge and vividness, that prose would find hard to rival, by Kirstein's deadly exact use of the profane vernacular and by his resourcefulness in the employment of rhyme—this is a feature of the whole collection—which, though carrying Byronic wit does not use the Byronic sesquipedelian method, achieving its effects through crackling brevity.

Stained-glass panels shed their red as in a
                chapel to endow
With rose reflection brass and bench, and
                bathe the bar in ruddy glow.
Exhausted though still unrelieved, some GI's
                lounge against the glass
To sip warm beer and drag dead butts and
                wait their rationed piece of ass.

Near two full hours before high noon but in
                this whore-home's smoky air
A stupified narcotic pulse vibrates the muzzy
                atmosphere.
Too bright and early to make love; nervous
                fatigue harasses haste.

We've just been dumped upon this town.
            We've fucking little time to waste,
And vice versa . . . .

The Anglo-Saxon monosyllables, the tabu on which has, of course, now been lifted for imaginative writers—often with doubtfully beneficial results—are fairly profusely scattered through Kirstein's verse, though 'scattered' is scarcely accurate since in fact they are carefully planted to convey colloquial realism an an ironic comment on the mindlessness of service profanity, as with that neat 'vice versa' quoted above.

The erotic element, that is a part of fear's extremity, appears less obviously in *Big Deal*. Major Marvin McGeek is a tall handsome man, 'A model of army-manual deportment and a common crook'. He is in charge of motor transport and doing well for himself in illicit deals with French civilians. He is also a coward, a condition shared by his subordinate, the ranker who narrates the poem and to whom McGeek says: 'I can spot guys with guts. I'm betting you are one.'

The poem continues:

Was he kidding? Marvin McGeek, wavy
            brunette, near six-foot-three,
Had not, as claimed, graduated from a good
            military academy
But indeed studied in schools of hard knocks
            and high kicks
Plus taking a few prizes in small percentages
            and the big fix.
I plead no moral or ethical advantage. It was clear
We'd caught the same nonfilterable virus: fear.

Later, during an air raid, the intensity of McGeek's fear is such that the enlisted man finds himself possessed by a temporary courage and he is able to lead his terrified and disoriented superior to the relative safety of the officer's billet. This aspect of fear and its opposite, familiar to every soldier who has known combat, the way in which the sickness of another's physical terror can lend to someone not naturally brave a temporary health of courage, or its simulacrum, is pinpointed with seemingly casual ease:

McGeek stumbled past my post; I presented
     him arms O.K.,
He, a stickler for ceremony, each detail done
     the rightway;
It was too dim to see me fumble in thick
     anticipatory gloom
While numerous indications promised
     imminent doom,
In zinc clouds, steely air, breathless X-ray
     stealth
Of buzz-saw noises inimical to human health.

'Hey, man,' he gasps, 'it's you.' I smell his
     musk of relief,
He more jittery than me. It takes thieves to
     catch a thief.
'I'm that pissed,' he moans, 'I'm blind.' A
     silly lie.
'You know where I live?' 'No, but show me,
     sir,' volunteer I.
'See me home, son.' It's an order? Do I
     abandon my post?
Is this a test or a trap? All indeed may be lost

Yielding to magnetic attraction in this genus
     of male.
His intensity betrays indiscreet need. I feel him
     quail
So my valour rises . . . .

It is, of course, no accident that Kirstein's imagery of fear is also redolent of sexuality: 'I smell his musk of relief', 'I feel him quail / So my valour rises.'

The narrator in another poem, *Guts*, sees in France a German tank destroyed, its occupants burnt alive, and he is reminded of an adolescent encounter with a girl whom he deflowers in his father's sedan, and what might seem at first sight an arbitrary correlation of events is convincingly and movingly justified in Kirstein's characteristically wry mediatation on courage, honour, and the common fate, shared by all men, friend and foe, of being human:

> One question, one answer, acquits us;
> Caught cheating, we only confess:
> 'Who the hell do you think you are, man?'
> 'No worse than that bloody mess.'
> They're dead and I'm living: it's nonsense.
> They're shattered; I'm whole: it's a lie.
> Between us, identification:
> I am you, men; and, men, you are I.
> Tests of failure, dishonour can hardly
> Be matters of all-out degree.
> Fresh earth will smother you sweetly;
> A warm bath can take care of me.
> Gruesome glimpses we stare down, maintain us,
>
> Sin and squalor partly appeased.
> Such scale bravery may even sustain us,
> Our psyches released or increased.
> We've endured the Worst That Can Happen.
> Hallelujah! There can't be much more,
> But the ghastly surprises of history
> Hide their inexhaustible store,
> And exams in a peace that we pray for
> Make dunces of scholars at war.

It is a paradoxical fact that Kirstein, whose poems are made with immense care and every one of which is dependent for its shape on a traditional English matrix, is the least 'literary' of war poets because every piece he composes is steadily focused on the physical facts of a war situation that any soldier would recognise as both particular and general in its authenticity and, in almost every case, his adaptation of formal techniques to embody the reality he is striving for conceals the art and craft through its very expertness. Fear, and especially fear of death, is something that every fighting serviceman has to contend with, and each must discover his own way of preparing himself to encounter 'the ghastly surprises of history'. One of the most obvious and widely practised methods of preparation is to rehearse in the imagination the worst of what might happen in fact. Kirstein has written a poem, *Foresight,* where he anticipates a possible way in which he might be killed and he advances the super-stitious belief or hope that, through foreseeing and enduring the event in his mind, the actuality will be evaded or delayed.

Foresight is wonderfully well-written. Each three-line stanza conforms to a fairly regular metrical pattern with the first and third lines consisting of five or six feet in which anaepests are counterpointed against iambics, and the second of a single trisyllabic line with varying stresses. The rhymes are precise and regular, the two long lines of each stanza rhyming as couplets except in the second and third stanzas where, for variety's sake, and to sustain the colloquial tone, the first line of Stanza II rhymes with the last of Stanza III and the last line with the first. What is most remarkable about the structure is that within its formality Kirstein commands, through syntax and phrasing, a rhythm that is nervous and hesitant, the movement of the verse proceeding with a panting urgency, with abrupt stops and starts, a rhythm which perfectly communicates the breath-catching fearsomeness of the envisaged ordeal.

> Previsioning death in advance, our doom is
> > delayed.
> I guess mine:
> I'm driving for some dumb officer on this
> > raid:
>
> I can't doubt his sense of direction, his perfect
> > right.

Still, he's wrong.
I hint we're too far front. Been warned plenty
                about this before.

Base far off. No lights may be shown. He
                starts to get sore.
Lost, our road.
He feels he's failed. Abruptly down drops
                night.

Anticipate panic: his, mine, contagions fear
                takes.
THIS IS IT.
Not good. I invoke calm plus prayer for both
                our sakes.

Calm makes sense. Prayer is less useful than
                gin or a smoke.
Where are we?
If this ass hadn't tried to crack his great big
                joke,

Pushing beyond where he knew well we were
                told to go,
We'd be safe.
Checking my estimate, my unvoiced I Told
                You So,

Granite bang-bangs blossom all over hell and
                gone.
Let me Out!
My foreseen fright swells, a warm swarm and
                we're sure done

In by Mistake, including his fright, faking him
                brave;
Me the same,
Making me clam tight when I oughta had the
                brains to save

Our skins, sparing official pride by baring my
fear:
(Please, sir. *Turn.*)
Sharing his shame with me, who, also, deserve
some. Oh dear,

It's too late. The end of two nervous careers,
Of dear me,
And him, dear doubtless to someone, worth
her dear tears.

That last stanza is especially effective, the play upon 'dear' and the final unsentimental recognition that the 'dumb officer' is to be mourned by those his death bereaves.

This muted note of tenderness is sounded quite frequently through *Rhymes of a P.F.C.* and it rescues the book as a whole from what some readers might otherwise have felt as a too heartless and brilliant glitter of verbal pyrotechnics, but it is not often overstated or romanticised. *Tent Mates,* for instance, is coolly realistic about the problems presented by the enforced intimacies imposed on all soldiers, particularly those serving in the ranks, and there is no lip-service paid to conventional notions of the value of comradeship and *esprit de corps.* Sentimentality does, perhaps, mar a few of the poems, and some of those in the *U.K.* section, which applaud British phlegm and Cockney humour, sometimes using awful sub-Kiplingesque phonetic spelling, read rather like public relations propaganda for wartime Anglo-American get-togetherness. Occasionally the demanding metres and rhyme-schemes, that Kirstein always uses, force upon his work a note of contrivance, monotony and even awkwardness, but these moments are infrequent and the wonder is that he has so successfully covered such a wide range of experience, ideas and emotions with unflagging invention and originality, from the wickedly funny (with overtones of sadness) *Gloria,* a lisping monologue of a homosexual in a wartime bar, to the thoughtful and moving poem on the victims of Hitler's Final Solution, *The Chosen.*

❋

I have discussed Lincoln Kirstein's work first in this survey of American war poetry, not because I regard him as necessarily the 'best' of the writers dealt with here, but because he is the one whose considerable talent has received least recognition. Randall Jarrell, who was born in Nashville, Tennessee, in 1914 and who served as a sergeant-pilot in the U.S.A.A.F., first operationally and subsequently as an instructor, has been widely regarded as having written some of the most memorable poems of the Second World War. His *Death of the Ball Turret Gunner* is among the most frequently anthologised poems to have come from battle experience in the 1939–45 war and it is one of the most bitter condemnations of war's waste and futility to have been written in the past half century or so.

All poetry about war in the twentieth century must be, to some degree, denunciatory (as Louis Simpson commented in the passage quoted earlier: 'Any true description of modern warfare is a protest . . .'), but not all war poets are equally or exclusively denunciatory; many, as this book should have shown, find something to celebrate or affirm, if it is only the intensity of response to emotional situations which, in time of peace, would have been taken for granted and whose poignancy scarcely felt, the anguish of farewell and separation, and the ecstasy of brief re-union with ones beloved, the enrichment of love and of life itself by the proximity of danger and possible— even probable—death, the value of courage and the consolations of comradeship, the unifying power of shared ordeals. Jarrell sees war as totally destructive and pointless, the circumstances wholly degrading, robbing the individual of all that separates him from the predatory beasts, an evil which in the natural harmony of things, achieving nothing. There are no victors in Jarrell's view of war, only victims, among whom he would number the survivors as well as those who, like the flak-smashed ball turret gunner, was '. . . washed . . . out of the turret with a hose.'

From my mother's sleep I fell into the State,
And I hunched in its belly till my wet fur
          froze.
Six miles from earth, loosed from its dream of
           life,

I woke to black flak and the nightmare
                                        fighters.
When I died they washed me out of the
                          turret with a hose.

Jarrell is an uneven poet, rarely dull but, in his wartime verse, quite often given to prolixity and he sometimes permits his language to clot, the violence and inconsistency of imagery to run riot, and he cannot always control a tendency to muddle the abstract and concrete so that, instead of the powerful statement he wishes to make, he obscures his subject and blurs his effects. At this stage in his poetic development he does not seem to have realised that the verb and noun are the muscle and bone of language and qualifying words—adjectives and adverbs—are the flesh. A too generous endowment of flesh leads, of course, to obesity, and some of Jarrell's earlier poetry of the war does seem overweight.

The carrier meshed in its white whirling wake,
The gray ship sparkling from the blue-black sea,
The little carrier—erupts in flak,
One hammering, hysterical, tremendous fire.
Flickering through flashes, the stained rolling clouds,
The air jarred like water tilted in a bowl,
The red wriggling tracers—colonies
Whose instant life annexes the whole sky—
Hunt out the one end they have being for,
Are metamorphosed into one pure smear
Of flame, and die
In the maniacal convulsive spin
Of a raider with a wing snapped off, the plane
Trailing its flaming kite's-tail to the wave.

At least six of the epithets in those few lines from *Pilots, Man Your Planes* are not only dispensable, their jettisoning would sharpen the visuality of the description and generally tauten the passage.

Here, in *Burning the Letters*, the widow of a pilot killed in action reflects, years after the event, on his death:

>   Here to my hands
> From the sea's dark, incalculable calm,
> The unchanging circle of the universe,
> The letters float: the set yellowing face
> Looks home to me, a child's at last,
> From the cut-out paper; and the licked
> Lips part in their last questioning smile.
> The poor labored answers, still unanswering;
> The faded questions—questioning so much,
> I thought then—questioning so little;
> Grew younger, younger, as my eyes grew old,
> As that dreamed-out and wept-for wife,
> Your last unchanging country, changed
> Out of your own rejecting life—a part
> Of accusation and of loss, a child's eternally—
> Into my troubled separate being.

Not only do we find in these lines a similar excess of adjectives but the qualifying words often predict clichés, near-clichés, or empty rhetorical flourishes: 'incalculable calm', 'unchanging circle of the universe', 'poor labored answers', 'faded questions' and so on. One feels that, far too often, Jarrell has found it necessary to pad out the pentameter with unnecessary verbal baggage. He is generally happier with the shorter line though in *A Pilot from the Carrier,* he handles the pentameter with much more assurance, he eschews the abstract and keeps his eye on the hard details, conveying the physical sense of the parachute descent with admirable skill:

> And falls, a quiet bundle in the sky,
> The miles to warmth, to air, to waking:
> To the great flowering of his life, the
>   hemisphere

That holds his dangling years. In its long slow
sway
The world steadies and is almost still . . . .
He is alone; and hangs in knowledge
Slight, separate, estranged: a lonely eye
Reading a child's first scrawl, the carrier's
wake . . . .

Among the many poems which deplore the inescapable reduction of man to either animal or instrument by the calculated process of military training and by the uniformed civilian's enforced acceptance of the murderer's role, the cruel larceny of all sense of personal identity, is *Mail Call*, and here Jarrell is at his formidable best. The scene-setting is masterly: the visual sharpness of the flung letters, the irony that sees each missive just escaping the clutching hand of its intended recipient; then the meditation which follows the initial imagic statement develops naturally and movingly to the conclusion with its haunting ambiguities: 'The soldier simply wishes for his name'. Quite literally he wants to hear his name called by the distributor of mail; perhaps less consciously, but no less urgently, he wishes to re-establish contact with the world beyond the limbo of army existence, to hear from some one to whom he is a name, a unique person, not just a number and a function: he 'wishes for his name' because he longs for the restoration of identity that has been stolen from him by his absorption into a military unit.

The letters always just evade the hand.
One skates like a stone into a beam, falls like
a bird.
Surely the past from which the letters rise
Is waiting in the future, past the graves?
The soldiers are all haunted by their lives.

Their claims upon their kind are paid in paper
That establishes a presence, like a smell.
In letters and in dreams they see the world.

They are waiting: and the years contract
To an empty hand, to one unuttered sound—
The soldier simply wishes for his name.

The theme of military man reduced to the level of animal or
object is often repeated or hinted at in other poems but it is only
in one, *Eighth Air Force,* which examines the condition of the
soldier whose humanity has been diminished and bestiality
fostered by his training and environment, that we find at least a
hint that he is not irredeemably reduced, that there might even
exist a certain nobility and self-sacrifice in his acceptance of his
role as killer, that traces of his former innocence and gentleness
remain, and, above all, he is not to be judged and condemned.

If, in an odd angle of the hutment,
A puppy laps the water from a can
Of flowers, and the drunk sergeant shaving
Whistles O *Paradiso*!—shall I say that man
Is not as men have said: a wolf to man?

The other murderers troop in yawning;
Three of them play Pitch, one sleeps, and one
Lies counting missions, lies there sweating
Till even his heart beats: One; One; One.
O *murderers*! . . . Still, this is how it's done . . .

The wolf, the murderer, cares for a puppy; there are flowers in
the water-can and the song whistled, however ironically or
thoughtlessly, is one of spiritual aspiration; a simple game is
played, a vestigial childness and simplicity persist; one of the
'murderers', who evidently has only one more mission to
complete before his operational tour is over, lies in an agony of
apprehension. The resolution of the poem is neither facile nor
consolatory. Jarrell half-accuses himself of lying—or of casuis-
tic self-justification—then bows to historical necessity in a
conclusion that is sadly resigned yet dignified:

Men wash their hands, in blood, as best they
can:
I find no fault in this just man.

In another poem, *Second Air Force,* images of men seen as beasts again appear but, to the soldier's mother, through whose eyes events are seen, the men are changed irrevocably to the less than human; both they and their planes are variants of the same destructive species:

       . . . . their Fortresses, all tail,
Stand wrong and flimsy on their skinny legs,
And the crew climb to them clumsily as bears.
And the green, made beasts run home to air.
The soldiers pass like beasts,
unquestioning . . . .

Apart from a couple of his rather weaker poems, *Transient Barracks* and *The Dead Wingman,* where there might be detected a faint glimmer of affirmation, in the first, a cautious and drab celebration of an airman's return to his homeland and, in the second, a recognition that personal affection and loyalty can survive the dehumanisation of service-life and combat conditions, Jarrell's war poetry becomes progressively more bitter and despairing. *The Range in the Desert* ends uncompromisingly:

Profits and death grow marginal:
Only the mourning and the mourned recall
The wars we lose, the wars we win;
And the world is—what it has been.

The lizard's tongue licks angrily
The shattered membranes of the fly.

In *The Lines* the soldiers are not even granted the status of animals: they are merely things:

After the center's naked files, the basic line
Standing outside a building in the cold
Of the late or early darkness, waiting
For meals or mail or salvage, or to wait
To form a line to form a line to form a line;
After the things have learned that they are
                              things,
Used up as things are, pieces of the plain
Flat object-language of a child or states;
After the lines, through trucks, through
                              transports to the lines
Where the things die as though they were not
                              things—
But lie as numbers in the crosses' lines . . . .

Here is the anguish of frustration and despair only just held back
from the wordless abyss by the order and discipline of art and
the controlling intelligence.

Field Hospital, a firmly moulded and verbally chaste poem,
ends with its subject, a wounded soldier, 'comforted', but the
comfort is that of oblivion and, from the pain and desperation
that informs so much of Jarrell's war poetry, the reader might
reasonably assume that, for the poet, dreamless sleep is the only
possible refuge from the senseless and destructive realities of
war.

He stirs, beginning to awake.
A kind of ache
Of knowing troubles his blind warmth; he
                              moans,
And the high hammering drone
Of the first crossing fighters shakes
His sleep to pieces, rakes
The darkness with its skidding bursts, is done.
All that he has known

Floods in upon him; but he dreads
The crooked thread

Of fire upon the darkness: 'The great drake
Flutters to the icy lake—
The shot-guns stammer in my head.
I lie in my own bed,'
He whispers, 'dreaming'; and he thinks to
                                        wake.
The old mistake.

A cot creaks; and he hears the groan
He thinks his own—
And groans, and turns his stitched, blind,
                        bandaged head
Up to the tent-flap, red
With dawn. A voice says, 'Yes, this one';
His arm stings; then, alone,
He neither knows, remembers—but instead
Sleeps, comforted.

Only rarely does Jarrell turn to the brief satirical poem but when he does he handles it with great accomplishment and I would have liked to have seen more of such sardonic pieces as *Gunner* (Has my wife a pension of so many mice? / Did the medals go home to my cat?') and *A War*:

There set out, slowly, for a Different World,
At four, on winter mornings, different legs . . .
You can't break eggs without making an omelette
—That's what they tell the eggs.

The war, which could be the First World War, the Second, or indeed any war in Jarrell's view, achieved nothing. In his reversal of the old adage, millions of eggs were broken—that is to say, millions of lives were lost—and the only consequence was incalculable suffering, humiliation and waste. There is no mistaking the intensity of Jarrell's pain, pity and despair nor the inflexibility of his truthfulness. There are moments in his war poetry when the force of his passion results in confusion and overstatement but far more frequently it is directed and controlled through a technical assurance that has produced some of the most relentless indictments of the evil of war since Sassoon and Owen.

Karl Jay Shapiro was born in Baltimore, Maryland, a year before Randell Jarrell in 1913. He was drafted into the Army in 1941 and the following year he was posted to the Pacific Area. His first collection—other than a privately printed volume of juvenilia—was *Person, Place and Thing,* published in 1942, and this was succeeded in 1944 by *V-Letter* which contains most of his poetry which derives from his experience as a soldier. *Person, Place and Thing,* however, contains one wartime poem, *Conscription Camp,* which impresses me more favourably than anything in the later book. Perhaps the poems in *V-Letter,* all written on active service, were too hurriedly composed in conditions inimical to creative work; whatever the reason *V-Letter,* as a whole, does not fulfill the real promise of *Person, Place and Thing,* though it does include four or five poems which deserve a place in any anthology of Second World War poetry.

Shapiro is a stylish writer with a commendable regard for his craft, but much of his work is vitiated by what comes across to the reader as a wish to charm. A great deal of his language and imagery possesses a fatal sweetness; he has something of W. H. Auden's poise and technical dexterity but he lacks Auden's sheer imaginative sweep, intellectual rigour and astringency that seldom permit sentimentality to corrupt the purity of the expression.

The poem I mentioned from *Person, Place and Thing, Conscription Camp,* shows Shapiro at his most restrained best. The description of the Virginian landscape is excellent and he allows, with apparent effortlessness, the actual phenomena to function as metaphor for the tired depression and ennui weighing down the spirits of the conscripted soldiers. In the last two quatrains he just manages to restrain his impulse towards rhetorical exaggeration in this evocation of sunset and the drafted recruits' sad and desperate pursuit of escape through temporary pleasure:

And like a very tired whore who stands
Wrapped in the sensual crimson of her art
High in the tired doorway of a street
And beckons half-concealed the passerby,

The sun, Virginia, on your Western stairs
Pauses and smiles away between the trees,
Motioning the soldier overhill to town
To his determined hungry burst of joy.

Aside, the first poem in *V-Letter*, takes as its central situation the same incident as Jarrell's *Mail Call*, the distribution among troops of letters from home but, although Shapiro's poem is longer and, on the surface, more complex, it lacks both the immediate force and the lingering resonances of *Mail Call* and its conclusion, self-consciously resolute, adopting a stance of stoical defiance, does not seem to have taken all the facts of war into account. The slackness and crude contrast of 'rose' and 'slime' are not reassuring and one is too readily reminded of the politician's exhortation in 'the blood of the sweat of our brow'. The syntax, with all those phrases starting with the preposition 'of', is extraordinarily clumsy for one who prides himself on technical accomplishment.

Say no more of the dead than a prayer, say no
more of the land
Where the body is lain in the coral than that
it is far;
Take your finger away from the map of
wherever-we-are,
For we lie in the map of the chart of your
elderly hand;
Do not hasten the future; in agony too there
is time
For the growth of the rose of the spirit astir
in the slime.

For aside from ourselves as we are there is
nothing alive

Except as it keeps us alive, not tomorrow
                                  but now,
Our mail-day, today of the blood of the
                        sweat of our brow,
The year of our war to the end. When and
                        where we arrive
Is no matter, but *how* is the question we
                        urgently need,
How to love and to hate, how to die, how to
                        write and to read.

Melbourne, a soldier's travel-note which turns at the end into a love poem, is very Audenesque with lines like 'The family's sex is English, and all their pain / More moderate than a long expected death', but, as so often in Shapiro's verse, the manner, so assured and confident, conceals a vagueness, a failure to think things through. I do not think I am being chauvinistic to object that 'The family's sex is English' does not make much sense. Presumably the poet means that typical Australians are inhibited by a birthright of Anglo-Saxon puritanism, repression, British reticence, emotional or sexual reserve and coldness, but this is a cliché attitude that needs more than mere statement if it is to carry conviction in a poem, and I am at a loss to understand why Shapiro should think that Australians are less susceptible to pain than anyone else.

Troop Train is a better poem than *Melbourne* though it is weakened by a sugariness of language that prompts mistrust of the strength of the emotional content:

                . . . . Business men
Glance hopefully and go their measured way.
And women standing at their dumbstruck door
More slowly wave and seem to warn us back,
As if a tear blinding the course of war
Might once dissolve our iron in their sweet
                                  wish.

And in *The Gun* the form and diction seem almost perversely

chosen to make the apprehension of his subject's reality virtually impossible. The gun—from internal evidence his rifle—is
seen in phallic terms as, I suppose, a post-Freudian writer must
see it, or at least take its symbolic significance into account.
Nothing wrong with this so long as the exploration of the
relationships between phallus and gun, the killer and his weapon,
is conducted rigorously and with a watchful eye on the external
realities involved; but the romantic poeticisms, the *fin de
siècle* imagery and rhythms, apart from the confusion in the
poem's argument, invalidate the whole thing and you feel that
neither you nor the poet has learnt anything about either
sexuality or guns.

Sunday: New Guinea is a much simpler poem and a far more
successful one. It is an account of a Church Parade on active
service abroad and its emotive charge comes from the fact that,
in rehearsing the remembered forms of religious observance,
recollections of home and the simple delights of civilian Sundays
are brought into shape and painful focus to the exiled soldiers.
It seems a pity that Shapiro had to overload the poem with the
last line of the last stanza:

> I long for lounging in the afternoons
> Of clean intelligent warmth, my brother's
> mind,
> Books and thin plates and flowers and shining
> spoons,
> And your love's presence, snowy, beautiful
> and kind.

One does not, of course, doubt the genuineness of feeling
behind the words, but, while the truest art is not necessarily 'the
most feigning', neither is sincerity of feeling any guarantee of
artistic effectiveness. Those three adjectives—'snowy, beautiful
and kind'—are not only feeble and imprecise but could have on
the reader an effect quite different from what the poet presumably intends. These carelessly applied epithets do not bring
the woman to life and make her seem to the reader lovable; on
the contrary her image is as vague and inert as the words

themselves and a second look at the adjectives does not restore confidence in Shapiro's artistry: 'snowy', which is not so far from 'frosty', could suggest coldness, even frigidity; 'beautiful' is so generalised as to have no meaning, except subjectively, and 'kind' with its connotations of a bestowing of favours, graciousness and perhaps condescension seems an odd way to describe the girl you love.

One of the most satisfactory poems in *V-Letter* is also one of the least personal. *Nigger* has a splendid energy of indignation that debars possible intrusion of the Shapiro sweetness and I am reminded of Lincoln Kirstein's work by its vigour and the way that Shapiro sustains an easy vernacular within the framework of the prescribed metre and exact rhyme-scheme.

> And did ever a man go black with sun in a
>   Belgian swamp,
> On a feathery African plain where the
>   sunburnt lioness lies,
> And a cocoanut monkey grove where the
>   cockatoos scratch the skies,
> And the zebras striped with moonlight grasses
>   gaze and stomp?
>
> With a swatch of the baboon's crimson
>   bottom cut for a lip,
> And a brace of elephant ivories hung for a
>   tusky smile,
> With the muscles as level and lazy and long as
>   the lifting Nile,
> And a penis as loaded and supple and limp as
>   the slaver's whip?
>
> Are you beautiful still when you walk
>   downtown in a knife-cut coat
> And your yellow shoes dance at the corner
>   kerb like a brand-new car,
> And the buck with the arching pick looks
>   over the new-laid tar
> As you cock your eye like a cuckoo bird on a
>   two-o'clock note?

When you got so little in steel-rim specs,
                    when you taught that French,
When you wrote that book and you made that
                    speech in the bottom south,
When you beat that fiddle and sang that role
                    for Othello's mouth,
When you blew that horn for the shirt-sleeve
                    mob and the snaky wench?

When you boxed that hun, when you raped
                    that trash that you didn't rape,
When you caught that slug with a belly of
                    of fire and a face of gray,
When you felt that loop and you took that
                    boot from a KKK,
And your hands hung down and your face
                    went out in a blast of grape?

Did the Lord say yes, did the Lord say no,
                    did you ask the Lord
When the jaw came down, when the cotton
                    blossomed out of your bones?
Are you coming to peace, O Booker T.
                    Lincoln Roosevelt Jones,
And is Jesus riding to raise your wage and to
                    cut that cord?

I must not give the impression that Shapiro always becomes
sentimental and diffuse when he is writing on personal themes.
Birthday Poem, for instance, is a fine piece of writing which
risks the direct statement of love, and through its intelligence
and well-calculated avoidance of solemnity and its comparative
chasteness of expression, it provides satisfaction and delight. It
is a war poem only because it is written by a soldier on active
service to the girl he loves and the presences behind the words,
the sense of vast separation, the threats of violence and death,
give an extra dimension of poignancy. The title-poem, *V-Letter,*
is a pleasing work of the same kind and it would be foolish to
underrate the quality of poems which speak directly of the

heart's affections in supple verse, without adopting a mask or
stance of detachment and irony. Here is the last stanza of
V-Letter:

> As groceries in a pantry gleam and smile
>   Because they are important weights
> Bought with the metal minutes of your pay,
> So do these hours stand in solid rows,
> The dowry for a use in common life.
>   I love you first because your years
> Lead to my matter-of-fact and simple death
>   Or to our open marriage,
> And I pray nothing for my safety back,
> Not even luck, because our love is whole
>   Whether I live or fail.

Finally we cannot complete a discussion of Shapiro's war
poetry without considering what must be his most ambitious
work in this genre, *Elegy for a Dead Soldier*. This is a fairly long
poem of eleven stanzas, each containing twelve iambic pentameters and conforming to a strict rhyme-sequence, the elegy
ending with a short epitaph of six lines. The first stanza presents
the scene of a burial service for a soldier killed in action; an
altar has been improvised on the tail-gate of a truck and the
dead man's comrades are gathered there for the short and
simple ceremony:

> A white sheet on the tail-gate of a truck
> Becomes an altar; two small candlesticks
> Sputter at each side of the crucifix
> Laid round with flowers brighter than the
>   blood,
> Red as the red of our apocalypse,
> Hibiscus that a marching man will pluck
> To stick into his rifle or his hat,
> And great blue morning-glories pale as lips
> That shall no longer taste or kiss or swear.

> The wind begins a low magnificat,
> The chaplain chats, the palmtrees swirl their
> > hair,
> The columns come together through the mud.

This is not bad writing but it is weakened by supererogatory and too hectically-coloured description: all that business about the flowers could surely have been done, and done better, in one line instead of six.

In the second stanza the poet's meditation on the death of his comrade begins with the recognition that a similar fate in all probability lies in store for the author, and indeed for all of the living congregated there, and the last lines ask rhetorically if death is as final as it seems or is there any hope of personal survival beyond the grave as promised by Christianity. No answer is attempted and the poem goes on to speak of the way in which every soldier in battle has foreseen his own death and, although statistically vast numbers of men are slaughtered, each man can only die once, so there is no essential difference between one death and many: the statistics are deceptive:

> However others calculate the cost,
> To us the final aggregate is *one*,
> One with a name, one transferred to the blest;
> And though another stoops and takes the gun,
> We cannot add the second to the first.

Shapiro contends that he is licensed to speak on behalf of his dead comrade by the fact that he has himself endured exactly the same fears as the soldier who has been killed and has even—as observer and, in his imagination, as victim—experienced the final ordeal of dying. The subject of the elegy was, it seems, a very ordinary man, non-political but reactionary in a thoughtless fashion, racially prejudiced, patriotic, optimistic and the kind of Christian who:

> . . . . never spoke of God. The Christmas tree,
> The Easter egg, baptism, he observed,
> Never denied the preacher on his perch . . . .

The epitaph that completes the poem states a conventionally hopeful homily, so unoriginal and unconvincing that one wonders at first how seriously it is meant. To describe the soldier as a Christian might seem intended as ironical, a preparation for further ironies, but the tone of the whole poem is grave, appropriately elegiac and within its limits thoughtful, so it is unlikely to change in its tiny postscript. Here is the Epitaph:

> Underneath this wooden cross there lies
> A Christian killed in battle. You who read,
> Remember that this stranger died in pain
> And passing here, if you can lift your eyes
> Upon a peace kept by a human creed,
> Know that one soldier has not died in vain.

Clearly no irony is intended and the banality of the epitaph lies also at the heart of the poem, the purpose of which seems to be palliative, and while it could be argued that such writing offered consolation to the bereaved in time of war it is not the business of poetry to offer comfort at the expense of truth. Randall Jarrell, in the five lines of *Death of the Ball Turret Gunner*, tells us more about death in battle than Shapiro's one hundred and thirty-eight lines of the *Elegy for a Dead Soldier*.

In *Elegy for a Dead Soldier*, and elsewhere in *V-Letter* apart from the personal statements of the love poems, one senses a curious lack of the poet's real involvement with his subject-matter, a lack which is emphasised rather than diminished by the frequent extravagance and sensuousness of language and imagery. Louis Simpson is a poet whose work is instinct with a strong lyric impulse which is exercised in his war poetry with exemplary discretion that precludes falsification of his apprehension of reality. Strictly speaking Simpson's poems about war do not come within the scope of this book for they were not written while he was a serving soldier, but to omit appraisal of them would be to ignore what are among some of the most effective poems to have had their source in their authors' experience of combat in the Second World War.

Simpson has said:[33]

'I enlisted in the US Army in 1943. A year later I was assigned to a glider-infantry regiment of the 101st Airborne Division, stationed in Britain. I served with the 101st in France, Holland, Belgium, and Germany. In combat I was a runner— that is, I carried messages. In Holland I was wounded by a shell fragment, and at Bastogne my feet were frost-bitten. I got through the war all right, but afterwards, when I was back in the States, I had a "nervous breakdown" and was hospitalized. I had amnesia; the war was blacked out in my mind, and so were episodes of my life before the war. When I left the hospital I found that I could hardly read or write. In these circumstances I began writing poems.

'Before the war I had written a few poems and some prose. Now I found that poetry was the only kind of writing in which I could express my thoughts. Through poems I could release the irrational grotesque images I had accumulated during the war; and imposing order on these images enabled me to recover my identity. In 1948, when I was living in Paris, one night I dreamed I was lying on the bank of a canal, under machine gun and morter fire. The next morning I wrote it out, in the poem "Carentan O Carentan", and as I wrote I realised that it wasn't a dream, but the memory of my first time under fire. So I began piecing the war together, and wrote other poems. "Memories of a Lost War" describes the early days of the fighting in Normandy; "The Battle", the fighting at Bastogne.'

Of the poems mentioned above I doubt if any would hold much attraction for the ordinary, uneducated enlisted man as Simpson hoped they would, for such a hypothetical reader would almost certainly be impressed by the meretricious as he usually is in other art forms. In fact *The Battle* is a wonderfully well-achieved and economical piece of writing, the restraint of which increases rather than reduces its emotive charge. The soldiers in the first quatrain are described as 'Helmet and rifle, pack and overcoat'. This is visually precise: from any distance, even a relatively short one, it is impossible to distinguish between one infantryman and another when they are moving into action; they are not people with recognisable characteristics, but shapes created by the accoutrements. But Simpson is doing more than painting an accurate picture; he is deliberately eliminating the human because, in battle, the human is almost irrelevant, the soldier becomes an extension of his equipment, or such is the aim of his conditioning. Yet humanity at a rudimentary level persists, if only in the body's suffering: 'Their feet began to freeze'. In the last quatrain, and for the first time, the individual, in the person of the poet himself, speaks. The shift from the impersonal third person plural to the first person singular is paralleled by a shift in tone, from a lens-cold objectivity to an involved but carefully restrained compassion.

> Helmet and rifle, pack and overcoat
> Marched through a forest. Somewhere up
> > ahead
> Guns thudded. Like the circle of a throat
> The night on every side was turning red.
>
> They halted and they dug. They sank like
> > moles
> Into the clammy earth between the trees.
> And soon the sentries, standing in their holes,
> Felt the first snow. Their feet began to freeze.
>
> At dawn the first shell landed with a crack.
> Then shells and bullets swept the icy woods.
> This lasted many days. The snow was black.
> The corpses stiffened in their scarlet hoods.
>
> Most clearly of the battle I remember
> The tiredness in eyes, how hands looked thin
> Around a cigarette, and the bright ember
> Would pulse with all the life there was within.

The tone of *Memories of a Lost War* is more obviously lyrical than that of *The Battle* but the lyricism is not forced, developing as it does quite naturally from the brutal images of the earlier lines which describe the havoc caused by mortar fire: '. . . burst boots and packs and teeth / That seem to smile.' Although the poem is written in the present tense one would know—apart of course from the title—that it was a retrospective work, because it posseses a dream-like quality, almost a serenity. This does not call into question its authenticity. The poem is not about the primary experience but about the experience recalled from some distance in time and the title is important. Why is the war described as 'lost'? Perhaps because all wars are lost—certainly they are for those who are killed in them—but more particularly this war, the poet's own unique war, its shattering immediacy, has already receded in time and altered its aspect, become a memory. But memory is not necessarily opposed to truth and the distant view can often perceive proportion and relations that would be imperceptible in close-up. The transition from night-mare to more friendly dream occurs in the fourth verse:

> Hot lightnings stitch the blind eye of the
> > moon,
> The thunder's blunt.
> We sleep. Our dreams pass in a faint platoon
> Toward the front.

And then the haunting and mellifluous cadences of the last lines:

> Sleep well, for you are young. Each tree and
> > bush
> Drips with sweet dew,
> And earlier than morning June's cool hush
> Will waken you.

> The riflemen will wake and hold their breath.
> Though they may bleed
> They will be proud a while of something death
> Still seems to need.

The other poem referred to by Simpson, *Carentan O Carentan*, is much more obviously an attempt to write a poem that '. . . would be . . . tolerable to men who had seen a good deal of combat and had no illusions' but I find it less effective than either *The Battle* or *Memories of a Lost War* and, despite or more probably because of its claim on the attention of the non-literary reader, it carries an air of contrivance, indeed of 'literariness'. The simple ballad form, deliberately clumsy rhymes and off-rhymes, lines such as 'Far away the guns did sound' with that obtrusive 'did', all help to give a slightly spurious tone so that the piece reminds you of a quite cleverly made but nevertheless obviously faked antique. Here are the opening quatrains:

> Trees in the old days used to stand
> And shape a shady lane
> Where lovers wandered hand in hand
> Who came from Carentan.
>
> This was the shining green canal
> Where we came two by two
> Walking at combat-interval.
> Such trees we never knew.
>
> The day was early June, the ground
> Was soft and bright with dew.
> Far away the guns did sound,
> But here the sky was blue.

I am, perhaps, being too hard on this poem, which is an attractive piece of writing, but I find Simpson's longish narrative poem, *The Runner*, far more interesting as an attempt to write a serious work of literature which might appeal to men who had been through the same experiences with which the work deals but would have no liking for poetry per se. Simpson writes a short prose introduction to the poem:

This is the story of a soldier of the 101st Airborne Division of the Army of the United States.

The Runner is fiction; the episodes and characters are imaginary. But the fiction is based on the following history.

On September 17, 1944, parachute and glider infantry of the First British Airborne Division, the American 82nd and 101st Airborne Divisions, and a Polish brigade, descended in eastern Holland, at Eindhoven, Grave, Nijmegen and Arnhem. Their object was to make a bridgehead across the Lower Rhine at Arnhem. The British Second Army would join them and advance from Arnhem into the plains of Northern Germany.

At Arnhem the British airborne troops were attacked by enemy units in overwhelming strength, and forced back across the river. The more fortunate Americans defended a corridor from Eindhoven to Nijmegen. The fighting, bitter at first, settled into a stalemate, and, with the coming of the rainy season, petered out entirely.

In mid-November the 82nd and 101st were drawn back to Rheims, to re-equip and get the drizzle out of their bones.

On December 17, they were alerted for combat. A German attack was developing in Belgium. The divisions were hurried by truck into the Ardennes, and on the night of December 19, the 101st were digging in around Bastogne.

The Runner is written in twelve substantial sections of varying lengths and its metrical base is the pentameter. There are scattered assonances, rhymes and pararhymes, used both internally and as line-endings, but these are too irregularly placed to prompt the ear to discern a phonetic pattern and the rhythmic movement and general aural flavour is that of blank verse, occasionally too blank in the way that led Wordsworth in *The Prelude* to utter commonplaces as if he were declaiming holy writ. One of the problems of writing a work of some length in blank verse, or something closely approximating to it, is to convey detailed information without giving an excessive weight and stateliness to the line, and failure can produce a comic pomposity. Simpson, especially in the earlier parts of his poem, does not always manage to avoid this; neither, in his efforts to escape the danger of the over-portentous does he always succeed in preventing the intrusion of tired descriptive phrasing—'a sickening drop', 'flat as a pancake',—and he can produce lines of sub-Wordsworthian bathos like: 'The day was hot, and Dodd began to sweat'. But when this has been said it remains to insist that *The Runner*, in its total effect, is a powerful and exciting work.

The story is one of a young soldier being tested in battle, failing—or partially failing—undergoing disgrace and humiliation, and finally recovering manhood and some dignity through self-redemption. Dodd, the protagonist, is the runner of the title: that is, the soldier detailed to carry messages during battle. He is better-educated and more articulate than the other enlisted men in his outfit and, as frequently happens in such circumstances, the recognition of his intellectual superiority causes suspicion and resentment among his comrades who treat him with hostility and real or assumed contempt. The first two sections of the poem describe the taking-off from an airfield in England of the American glider division in which Dodd serves and we follow the flight of his particular aircraft to the battle-ground in Holland. Evidently Dodd has experienced combat before, in Normandy, and as his glider approaches its destination the remembrance of the terror of battle, which had been alleviated by the anodynes of non-combat soldiering and by the repeated talk of past ordeals, that verbalizing whose purpose it is to veil the reality rather than recapture it, the true remembrance returns.

> Now he remembered. And it seemed unjust
> That he should be required to survive
> Again. The sound increased. The battleground
> Looked ominous. Visions of a huge mistake
> Struck at his heart.

The next five sections of *The Runner* give a vivid account of the fighting, culminating in Dodd's accomplishing the useful job of supplying the mortars with ammunition and receiving a few commendatory and friendly words from one of the mortar-crew, an occurrence which gives him great satisfaction:

> . . . . 'You're a good man, Dodd.'
>   That night he lay

> Smiling, without a care, beneath the sky.
> He had done all that could be expected.

But Dodd's moment of modest triumph and self-satisfaction is short-lived. In the eighth section of the poem the runner is returning on a moonlit night to his own unit having been on some unspecified errand and, in order to avoid a field of putrefying corpses left unburied from an earlier and violent skirmish, he takes another path which he believes will lead him back to his Company's position but his sense of direction betrays him and he stumbles into a detachment of Germans. Terrified, he turns and runs for his life, pursued by enemy small-arms fire, and in his desperate flight he drops his rifle; blindly he runs on until:

> . . . . He stumbled, reeled,
> And fell. His helmet flew off with a clang.
>
> Feet were approaching. He lay still as death.
>
> 'It's Dodd,' said a voice.
>
>   At last, he looked up
> Into the faces of the third platoon.
> Fisher. Others. They looked down in wonder.

After this incident we see Dodd's outfit resting under canvas near Rheims and the runner has become the mercilessly harassed butt of his Company, its resident clown, but not a clown to be regarded indulgently or affectionately. His wild running from danger and the losing of his rifle have proved him contemptible, so the resentful dislike the other men have always felt for what they took to be his affectation of superiority has now been sanctioned. He is treated no better by officers or N.C.O.s and is given the most unpleasant and degrading duties to perform, the digging of latrines, picking up litter around the camp and cleaning the greasy kitchen utensils after meals. In this, the ninth and longest section of *The Runner*, his humiliation and misery are painfully communicated; then follows an account of a dream enjoyed by Dodd which, in some way not quite clear either to Dodd himself or to at least one reader of the poem, is significant and consoling. After his dream, the runner climbs a slope to a vantage-point overlooking Rheims and there he experiences a kind of waking vision:

> He lit a cigarette. Then, near at hand,
> He saw the earth was trenched. A long
> > depression,
> No more than a foot deep, with rotten posts
> And scraps of wire, wound across the slope.
> He stood, and walked along it. The earth gave
> Under his boots. He picked up a small scrap
> Of wire, and it crumbled. He surmised
> This was a trench dug in the first Great War.
> Who knew? Perhaps an older war than that.
> He faced the East, to Germany and Russia.
> Shadows were standing with him. It was cold.
> They watched, wrapped in old overcoats,
> > forgotten.
> They stamped their feet. The whole world was
> > deserted
> Except for them; there was nobody left.
> On the imagined parapet, a cross
> Howled in the wind; and there were photo-
> > graphs
> Of girls and children; bunches of cut flowers.
> Then, on the pitted, gaunt escarp, the night,
> The melancholy night, swept with grandeur.
> Far in the dark, star-shells were blossoming.
> They stamped their feet. It was too cold. Too
> > much
> To expect of them. Their boots sank in the
> > mud.
> Their veins seemed ice; their jaws creaked
> > with the cold.
> They spoke; their words were carried on the
> > wind,
> Mingled, and lost.

The implications of both the sleeping and the waking reveries would seem to be that Dodd's personal failure, unhappiness, even his ultimate fate are diminished almost to irrelevance when seen against the enormous totality of suffering and loss inflicted by the war in which he is involved and even more diminished when set against the infinitely vaster canvas of the wars of the past, and the realisation of this reconciles him to his present condition. Then the present supervenes as he becomes aware of activity in the camp below. The company is preparing to move. He hurries back to rejoin his comrades:

> Dodd took his place
> In the line of olive-drab, the overcoats,
> Helmets, packs, the gloved hands holding
> weapons.
> The roll was called; he answered to his name.
>
> They marched up to the trucks.
>
> 'Mount up!'
>
> He climbed
> Into the truck, and was packed in. The gate
> Clanged shut behind him.

The next two sections of *The Runner* describe the company moving towards Bastogne and preparing, in the first snowfall of the year, for the massive attack which the Germans are about to launch. The threatened assault occurs and Simpson's description of combat here must rival any other account of battle in either the verse or prose of the Second World War: he does not attempt to achieve his effects through elaborate or dramatic imagery but by using a language that is absolutely direct, unadorned, as steely and functional as the armaments he is observing in action, and by manipulating the pentameter so that the violent, spasmodic and unpredictable nature of what is happening is reflected in the movement of the verse. This is a poetry of precision and understatement as is no more clearly demonstrated as in the last sentence in the following extract:

> The tank was growing large.
> The cannon flashed. Machine-gun tracers
>   curved
> Toward it, and played sparkling on the steel.
> Still it came on, glittering in return
> From its machine guns. Then, a crashing flame
> Struck it, leaving a trail of smoke in air.
> The tank shuddered. It slewed broadside
>   around.
>
> Inside the plates, as on an anvil, hammers
> Were laboring. It trembled with explosions,
> And smoke poured out of it.
>   The slope was still,
> Sprawling with hooded figures—and the rest
> Gone back into the trees. Then there began
> The sound of the wounded.

In the ordeal of this battle Dodd behaves creditably and the final section of the poem opens with a short but superbly realised portrayal of the battlefield and its dead which shows that Simpson possesses an almost unequalled gift for capturing that strange, blood-freezing beauty that is peculiar to the landscape of war:

> Sometimes the snow came drifting down again.
> And when it ceased, eddies and gusts of wind
> Would lift it in long skirts that swept across
> The dead. It packed into the stiffened folds
> Of clothing. When night fell, a freezing wind
> Encased the tree-trunks in bright sheaths of
>   ice
> And hung bright icicles on every branch,
> And clamped the dead in rigid attitudes.

This momentary stillness is shattered, inevitably, by an artillery bombardment. The First Sergeant comes to Dodd's foxhole and gives the runner an important message to take to Battalion Headquarters. The ending is not overdramatised or sentimentalised, but the import is clear: Dodd has been redeemed, though there is a nice irony in the 'seemed to be' in the last line of the poem, an irony that offers no guarantee of eternity for his redemption:

> He slung his rifle over his right shoulder
> And climbed out of his hole.
>
>   'Keep out of trouble,'
> The sergeant said. 'Don't stop for anything.'
> Dodd started to move off. The sergeant
>   grasped
> His arm: 'Watch out! They may have got
>   patrols
> Between us and Battalion. Good luck!'
>
> Dodd waved his hand, although it was too
>   dark
> For the other to see him. And set off
> In what seemed to be the right direction.

The Runner, as I briefly indicated earlier, is not a faultless work but it is rarely dull and it offers many passages of great strength and beauty. It is also an unusual poem, especially from such a writer as Louis Simpson whose poetic strategies are generally about as far from the business of prose as it is possible to get, unusual because it is very close—some might say perilously close—to being a short story cast in verse. The question at once arises: what does it gain, if anything, in taking the form adopted? I think the gains are considerable.

Despite what Simpson says in the prose epigraph to his poem:—'*The Runner* is fiction; the episodes and characters are imaginary'—the reader may find in the poet's autobiographical prose book, *Air With Armed Men*, a prose account of the episode in which Dodd feeds the mortar-crew with ammunition, (the part of Dodd is played by Simpson himself) and a number of other scenes and occasions which find their place in the poem, and there is no doubt that, for immediacy, vividness and excitement, the poetry has it over the prose. The fact that a preformalised pattern is being imposed on the rhythms of ordinary speech tends to make the poet continuously more sensitive to the sonant possibilities of his language, technique forces him to weigh every syllable in a way that few, if any, prose-writers do, and the poet gains in being able to bring off ellipses and temporal leaps that would look distinctly odd, if not absurd, in a prose context, and he can modulate from fairly plain narration or description to the lyrical and to rich, even highly rhetorical bravura passages without causing in the reader an embarrassing sense of dislocation.

It is true that the poet suffers a concomitant disadvantage if he avails himself, for the sake of narrative continuity and clarity of the apparatus of the prose-writer, for he can then himself fall into another kind of absurdity:

'Dodd!'

He unzipped his bag, put on his helmet,
And stood.

'Where are you?'

It was the First Sergeant.
'Here,' the runner answered.

'Take this message
Back to Battalion. Are you listening?'

'Yes,' he said.

That one is able to scan these lines provides no alchemy for changing them from prose into poetry; on the contrary the versification leads the eye and ear to expect the resonances of poetry and instead they are given a bit of prose at its most banal. Simpson would have been much better served by a single line of indirect speech.

Still, *The Runner*, taken as a whole, is certainly not a failure and, although it was written twelve years after the war, I feel it deserves a place with his shorter works among the best poetry written by Americans who served their country in one or other of the fighting forces.

❈

All of the American poets so far discussed wrote from first-hand experience of what it was like actually to fight in the Second World War, either in the air or on land or—as in the case of the airborne infantryman, Louis Simpson—both in the sky and on the ground; if, as poets, they have anything in common it is a shared resolve to speak the truth about their reactions to the situation of being pressed into the role of killer and of being forced to live under the threat of imminent and violent death or maiming. During the First World War the intense pressure of circumstances insisted that Sassoon and Owen should each in his way forge for himself a new style to enable him to write honestly and directly about the unprecedented events in which he was engulfed, and it was at least partly from their examples that the poets of the second war found themselves already prepared with a means of dealing with their experiences. Those poets, British or American, who were actively involved in the fighting were not primarily concerned with theories of literature but with getting it down on paper and getting it right. There was no question of the search for 'objective correlatives'; most of the poetry of either war that is any good is faithful to the facts of what was happening and unlikely to be concerned with generalisation and abstraction. When Wilfred Owen made his famous statement: 'Above all I am not concerned with Poetry. My subject is War, and the pity of War. The Poetry is in the pity,' he meant that it would be idle for the poet to attempt to interpret events; he must simply record them as accurately as possible, for what happens in war, the events themselves, are charged with such intensities of terror, suffering, sacrifice and even beauty that the poetic imagination must abdicate in favour of the objective eye and the craftsman's hand.

The situation of Richard Eberhart during the Second World War was rather different from that of the aforementioned poets: for one thing, though he was in the U.S. Naval Reserve (in which he held the rank of Lieutenant Commander) he served as an instructor and did not experience battle, and for another he was considerably older than most of the poets who served in the war and was already an established author with three published collections of verse to his credit and he had mastered a poetic technique and had come to hold certain philosophical and aesthetic convictions which set him apart from his younger contemporaries. Nevertheless he wrote a short poem which, almost by accident it seems, has become one of the best-known and widely anthologised works by an American Second World War poet. Of this poem Eberhart himself has written:[34]

'Of the several war poems I wrote during the Second World War "The Fury of Aerial Bombardment" has been most studied, and perhaps it is enough for me to say a few words about that poem. It was written in Dam Neck, Virginia, in the summer of 1944 while I was stationed there as a Naval Reserve officer teaching aerial free gunnery. I taught tens of thousands of young Americans to shoot the .50 calibre Browning machine gun from aircraft. The subject was called Sighting. All too soon their names would come back in the death lists. This depressed me so much that one time I was sitting on a barracks steps at the end of the day and felt the ruthlessness and senselessness of war so acutely that I wrote the first three stanzas of the poem, which are in effect a kind of prayer. I put it away. Sometimes later I felt it needed something added to it. Maybe the interval was a week or two. With an analytical mind, quite removed from the passionate one of the first three stanzas, I composed the last four lines. It is said that these in relation to the others make this a particularly modern poem. Indeed, if I had not added the last stanzas, perhaps the poem would remain unused.'

And here is the poem, *The Fury of Aerial Bombardment*:

> You would think the fury of aerial
>   bombardment
> Would rouse God to relent; the infinite
>   spaces

Are still silent. He looks on shock-pried faces.
History, even, does not know what is meant.

You would feel that after so many centuries
God would give man to repent; yet he can kill
As Cain could, but with multitudinous will,
No farther advanced than in his ancient furies.

Was man made stupid to see his own
                            stupidity?
Is God by definition indifferent, beyond us all?
Is the eternal truth man's fighting soul
Wherein the Beast ravens in its own avidity?

Of Van Wettering I speak, and Averill,
Names on a list, whose faces I do not recall
But they are gone to early death, who late in
                            school
Distinguished the belt feed lever from the belt
                          holding pawl.

Eberhart is quite right in thinking that, without the last stanza, the poem would have been, not only incomplete, but of comparatively little interest. The first three quatrains are well written enough and their rhetoric has its moments of power, but the content is too generalised, too far removed from the facts of the subject with which it is supposed to be contending. It is the last stanza that makes the poem as a whole so effective: the three interrogatives hammered out with increasing urgency in the third stanza demand an answer, inviting one couched in their own metaphysical terms. No answer is supplied in the final four lines. Instead, Eberhart comes down from the upper regions of abstract speculation to the plain earth where ordinary men who lived and prematurely died are remembered, and the language becomes very simple, concrete, stripped of decoration and, in the last line, technical, so that the questions that have been posed in the preceding quatrain seem now not so much unanswerable as irrelevant.

I am not at all sure that this was Eberhart's intention. Elsewhere in his war poetry he seems profoundly concerned with problems of moral theology and curiously out of touch with the realities involved in the fighting of a war. He has written:[35]

> 'The poetry comes out of the chaos. Chaos is present to the poet in war in violent forms. He may recognize in this violence his true element, a reduction to terrible simplicity of what he knew in the heart before. Gigantic objectifications tossed and forced on sky, land and sea only emphasize the essential fact of struggle. Thus, a poet knows war without objective war in the world; it was conflict at the root of his mind that impelled him to the masking of these conflicts in the apparent resolution and order of works of art. In a dialectical sense, all poetry is war poetry.'

What Eberhart is saying here might seem dialectically persuasive but it suffers from the weakness that reduces much of his wartime poetry: the argument is conducted at a level which fails to take into account the extremity of war as known by the man who is directly embroiled, the sustained extremity of passion that the man is savaged by, the pain, fear, disgust and perhaps excitement and even exhilaration whose excessiveness and relentlessness render his world unrecognisably different from the world not at war: if all poetry is war poetry then all life must be war life and this, in any pragmatic sense, is manifestly untrue. In war the sheer magnitude of the conflict, the way in which it dwarfs the conflicts of peacetime existence, makes the whole fabric of existence strange, unnatural, and the only way for the poet to pin down the nature of that strangeness is by concentrating on the particular.

In Eberhart's poem, *Brotherhood of Man*, we see his attempt to universalise the particular in an imaginary account of the heroic defence of Corregidor. This fairly long poem is written in a form which derives from Anglo-Saxon alliterative verse (probably by way of Ezra Pound) and this lends at once what is presumably an intentionally archaic tone. Here is an account of the fighting:

Came wild men at each other, held off
                                  attackers,
Some slit the throats of the dead,

Drank the blood outright, howled wailing,
Slit the wrists of the living, others
With knives, or with fangs ravenous,
I saw them drinking the blood of victims,
Hell I was in, this was immitigable Hell.
Endless hours fought off famished, crazed
                              attackers.
Savage the senses in dreams of delirium,
Never knew how I surrendered not,
Saw clearly my mother in the midst of terror:
'Persevere. Persevere. Persevere. Persevere.'
Faith beyond reason, wrecked beyond words,
I dogged clung, daft before danger,
Dazed by disaster, damned in the hold.

Now, in this representative extract, Eberhart is obviously not aiming at a realistic portrayal of twentieth-century battle. The metre, the syntax and diction are all consciously of, not so much a previous age as a literary non-age, and the poet's intention to write about a specific historical event, yet convey intimations of previous wars, of war itself and its timeless universality, simply does not succeed. Kirstein, Jarrell or Simpson, focusing on the particular object and particular moment and using the speech rhythms and idioms of their day, come much closer to enshrining the timelessness, the universality of war, for the truth of the fact, of the actual is ungainsayable and it applies equally to Agincourt and Malplaquet as to Normandy and Salerno.

When Eberhart does explore a simple incident from his own experience of war, as in *Dam Neck, Virginia*, he can write delicately and movingly on one of the mocking paradoxes of technological warfare, the way in which killing weapons and those who control them are able to create appearances of strange beauty. Here he describes anti-aircraft guns firing tracers at night and his generalising conclusion is perfectly acceptable, following as it does from his primary response to the physical object:

They do not know the dream-like vision
                              ascending

In me, one mile away: they had not thought
                                        of that.
Huddled in darkness behind their bright
                                    projectors
They are the scientists of the skill to kill.

As this sight and show is gentle and false,
The truth of guns is fierce that aims at death.
Of war in the animal sinews let us speak not,
But of the beautiful disrelation of the spiritual.

Another successful war poem by Eberhart is *A Ceremony by the Sea*, a dignified and well-observed piece of work which obliquely laments the waste of war, but his violent frontal attack on the futility and evil of war in *At the End of War* begins and ends in near-hysterical rant. Here are the closing lines:

May they be woken up, blasted late,
Or reduced to eternal silences,
But may, pray God Almighty,
Man the cocky fighter,
The stupid and the self-destroyer,
The selfish and the vain,
The harmful cheater
The malicious debater,
The incurable self-lover
And the boring warrior,
The simpleton killer
May he learn humility
May humility be insinuated
More subtly than evil
Which brought ruin rocking him

May he turn the other cheek
Not bitten yet by worm of hate
May joy be his abandonment
In Thy forgiveness early and late

> And may he learn not to fight
> And never to kill, but love,
> Never, never to kill, but love,
> May he see Thy holy light.

Well, yes, but many of those who fought, dourly, reluctantly, and were maimed or killed, were not 'Cocky fighters' or especially selfish or vain, and if they had all turned the other cheek it would undoubtedly have been smashed in by a jack-boot. The total lack of wit and the holier-than-thou complacency of this poem are distinctly repellent.

In the prose statement from which I quoted earlier Eberhart has written[36] 'The war may present or force a subject; it may bring out a poet, or shock him into insensibility of silence. It may kill him. Or germinate the best war poems for exfoliation years after the event.' We have seen in the work of Louis Simpson that this later exfoliation did occur as it did in various forms with a number of American poets one of whom, Anthony Hecht, has written a work called *Drinking Song* which deals with the private defences the soldier in battle employs to make tolerable to himself his role as liberator and marauder, protector and killer.

Although *Drinking Song* is written in the present tense, about a particular time and place in the war, it could not, by the nature of its strategy and form, have been composed at the time of the events described. Hecht shows a platoon—or the remnants of a platoon—who have captured a German house of some size and magnificence, perhaps a castle, which has formerly been used to billet enemy troops. Here, the GIs find a supply of cognac and they drink recklessly to anaesthetise themselves against the fear and grief induced by the loss of five of their number 'dead in the pasture'. But the poet-narrator does not find liquor alone a sufficient anodyne; he adopts a mock-heroic stance, dramatising and romanticising his role, referring to his sub-machine gun as *Durendal*, the sword of Roland, and making use of a language that is decorous, slightly archaic in its phrasing:

> And *Durendal,* my only *Durendal,*
> Thou hast preserved me better than a sword;

Rest in the enemy umbrella stand
While that I measure out another drink.
I am beholden to thee, by this hand,
This measuring hand. We are beholden all.

Drinking Song does not offer the same sense of immediacy as a poem written during or soon after the event with which it deals, nor does it aim simply at the direct communication of what it was like to live through a moment of war. Its extreme formality and its stylishness impose an order on the original experience, and the raw events undergo a metamorphosis, they become curiously dream-like and ceremonious, and here Hecht shows not merely that alcohol—especially taken by men in a condition of acute strain and exhaustion—causes a sense of unreality (the slightly drunken speech-patterns and the partially glazed solemnity are beautifully caught without reducing the poem's seriousness) but that this state, even without the aid of any stimulant, is endemic in battle, perhaps in all situations of grave danger. *Drinking Song* has its own kind of realism but it is one which could be achieved only after the poet has distanced himself from the primary experience.

Howard Nemerov, who was born in 1920, a couple of years before Hecht, is also a writer of great stylistic accomplishment and one who also, I would guess, has been influenced by the practice and theories of John Crowe Ransom as Hecht most certainly has been. Although Nemerov served with both the Royal Canadian and the U.S. Air Forces he published very little verse which takes war directly for its subject. One poem, however, which does, *A Fable of the War*, is a remarkably controlled and elegant piece of writing, especially for a poet who was still in his twenties, and it is by no means lacking in profundity of feeling and thought, but it is oddly detached in its formality and possesses something of the dream-like quality of *Drinking Song*.

A Fable of the War describes a detachment of soldiers in transit, waiting at night 'Under a frame of blue glass and emptiness / In a station whose name I do not know'. The poet sees in the moonlight:

That we are dead. By stormless Acheron
We stand easy, and the occasional moon
Strikes terribly from steel and bone alike.

The soldiers are dead in a metaphysical sense: they are death's
men, committed to killing or being killed, and their spectral
aspect may be a premonitory indication of their fate. Then the
poem moves away from the actual scene to meditate upon its
significance:

But I have read that God let Solomon
Stand upright, although dead, until the temple
Should be raised up, that demons forced to
                          the work
Might not revolt before the thing was done.
And the king stood, until a little worm
Had eaten through the stick he leaned upon.

So gentlemen—by greatcoat, cartridge belt
And helmet held together for the time—
In honourably enduring her we seek
The second death. Until the worm shall bite
To betray us, lean each man upon his gun
That the great work not falter but go on.

The faintly archaic rhetoric of the last stanza, particularly the
last sentence with the inversion of 'lean each man upon his gun',
invites an ironic or at least partly ironic interpretation of the
reference to 'the great work', and here it anticipates the slightly
ambiguous, mocking tone of *Drinking Song*.

Of the poems whose source lies in the experience of war, the
one for which Nemerov is perhaps best known is not strictly a
war poem but one that deals with the immediate aftermath of
the conflict and shows, for the man who has been immersed in
the war, as indeed in any prolonged and violently traumatic
situation, how the past refuses to be buried but pervades and
may even displace the present. This poem, *Redeployment*, is

entirely different in tone from *A Fable Of War*: the grave, almost hieratic style has given way to a laconic conversational manner, though the poem's structure is not quite as casual as a superficial reading might suggest. The five line stanzas are unrhymed, but there are cunningly placed internal rhymes and assonances which provide subdued but pleasing harmonies.

> They say the war is over. But water still
> Comes bloody from the taps, and my pet cat
> In his disorder vomits worms which crawl
> Swiftly away . . . .

The poem concludes:

> The end of the war. I took it quietly
> Enough. I tried to wash the dirt out of
> My hair and from under my fingernails,
> I dressed in clean white clothes and went to
> bed.
> I heard the dust falling between the walls.

This is splendidly economical writing, the sense of menace, of lurking neurosis, evoked without fuss, and the more powerfully because of that.

Richard Wilbur, who was born in 1921 and fought in France and Germany with the 36th Infantry, belongs, with Hecht and Nemerov, to that school of poetry which enlisted most of the outstanding talents of the generation which came of age around the time of Pearl Harbour, the school which would have traced its origins back to the English metaphysical poets of the seventeenth century and would have vigorously rejected any paternity claims from Walt Whitman, eschewing free forms, expansive verbal gesticulations and the exclusive use of the idioms and rhythms of demotic speech in favour of wit, lucidity, grace and traditional prosody. Wilbur has chosen to preserve only a couple of poems which bear directly on his war experience,

Mined Country and *First Snow in Alsace*, both of which are beautifully made and unusual in that they reach without strain into regions of thought and feeling beyond the limits of their physical settings.

Mined Country begins with a finely etched scene of the landscape and soldiers moving cautiously over the innocent-seeming fields with their mine-detectors searching for the explosives planted just below the surface of the earth to blow the unwary to smithereens. Then the theme of man's obscene violation of nature is developed:

> Danger is sunk in pastures, the woods are sly,
> Ingenuity' s covered with flowers!
> We thought woods were wise but never
> Implicated, never involved.
>
> Cows in mid-munch go splattered over the sky;
> Roses like brush-whores smile from bowers;
> Shepherds must learn a new language; this
> Isn't going to be quickly solved.

In the penultimate stanza Wilbur moves away from the actual fields and woods to place the experience in the broader context of the whole of human existence, and the grave and tender counsel of the ending has that unpredictable inevitability that can be produced only by a poetic imagination of the first order:

> Sunshiny field grass, the woods floor, are so
>   mixed up
> With earliest trusts, you have to pick back
> Far past all you have learned, to go
> Disinherit the dumb child,
>
> Tell him to trust things alike and never to stop
> Emptying things, but not let them lack
> Love in some manner restored; to be
> Sure the whole world's wild.

In *Mined Country* Wilbur is concerned with extracting something of value, a hard-won wisdom, from an experience which, at first sight, would seem to be totally unedifying, and it seems to be his purpose to seek for the small redemptions and epiphanies in the vast nightmare of war, to perceive and give permanence to the fugitive moments of beauty and affirmation that gleam occasionally in the darkness of a world in conflict. *First Snow in Alsace*, less complex in thought than *Mined Country*, is full of splendidly observed detail:

> The ration stacks are milky domes;
> Across the ammunition pile
> The snow has climbed in sparkling combs.
>
> You think: beyond the town a mile
> Or two, this snowfall fills the eyes
> Of soldiers dead a little while.

The poet thinks of how 'At children's windows, heaped, benign, / As always, winter shines the most . . .' and the sense of innocence, of which the snow is emblematic, is briefly reawakened in the heart of the soldier:

> The night guard coming from his post,
> Ten first-snows back in thought, walks slow
> And warms him with a boyish boast:
>
> He was the first to see the snow.

As was the case in Britian during the Second World War, so in the United States there were many poets of lesser accomplishment and reputation than those we have so far examined who yet produced a considerable amount of respectable and sometimes memorable verse. William Jay Smith, who served in the U.S. Naval Reserve in the Pacific and in European waters, wrote some very pleasing poems based on his service life in wartime, works such as the jaunty and tough *Hotel Continental* and *Convoy*, and the original and rather moving *Today I Have Touched The Earth*, with its splendid repeated line, 'I address you from the wardroom of the Whale'. *Morning at Arnhem*, too, has some passages of neat observation and the emotional content is not allowed too free a rein, though its presence is tellingly there:

In Holland there are tulips on the table,
A wind from the north on the grey stones
That breaks the heart, and sits upon the
                              shoulder,
And turns the mill, the pine cones.

Waking below the level of the sea,
You wake in peace; the gardens look
Like roofs of palaces beneath the water,
And into the sea the land hooks.

In Holland there are tulips on the table,
A wind from the north on the grey stones
That breaks the heart, and turns, with the mill
                              at cockcrow,
Over the quiet dead, the pine cones.

Two other Navy poets, Louis O. Coxe and Hubert Creekmore, both wrote well on the theme or erotic love and its mutations in time of war, Coxe the more hopefully in *Pin-Up Girl*:

The heart in camera takes its symbols from
Possession, love, and childhood and collects
Pictures of scrapbook happiness, glued next
To blurred prints from the negatives of home
And mine, that built on symbols, is perplexed
To find you where it hid a bolted room.

Creekmore writes with bitter resignation in *Pocket Guide for Servicemen* of the diminution and distortion of love:

> Here the pioneering spirit finds
> Its last debased residence, and blind
> To honor, honors nothing.
>
> It is too late to teach a fighter love
> When he must kill. It is too much to build
> Respect where none has been, or been owed.

And each has his savage anti-war poem. Coxe in *Dead Marine*:

> This is the death by water. This is dying
> Bloat and fishbelly white a thing that slips
> And slobbers on the groundswell. Denying
> This to survival is the final lying
> Before witnesses . . . .

and Creekmore in *Dividends*, where a stricter form might have controlled the surging indignation more effectively than the free verse he employs:

> We are bringing back some cancelled notes.
> We have them here on the deck, in the bright
> > sun,
> With aluminium smears of ocean writhing
> > under the heated clouds.
> This is a sort of report to the stockholders.
> Each figure on the diagram represents one
> > thousand.
>
> Item: a sailor, leg cut off.
> Credit: votes for irresponsible politicians.
> Item: a soldier, right arm missing.

Credit: copy and blurbs for conscienceless
                                    journals.
Item: a marine, face gone.
Credit: . . . .

All three of these sailor-poets wrote generally in prescribed
forms and their work possesses the virtues of the prevailing
orthodoxy of their time, clarity, intelligence and a watchful
reticence. Auden is probably the principal influence, as he
certainly is on the war poetry of John Ciardi, who was an air-
gunner in the U.S. Air Force, but Ciardi contributes an individual lyric note which is all his own and he writes with unusual
skill and assurance for a poet who was then still in his twenties.

And all night long from window sills
The Angels beckoned and the bills
Of visors turned and made their kills.

We burned like kisses on the night,
And talented and drunk and bright
We shed ourselves in coloured light.

Because the train was at the gate,
And clocks were closing down the date,
And all the seas were running late.

And in *Camptown* we find him handling a more complex stanza
with equal smoothness:

Whirling on the sidewalk, eddying the street,
Dammed where the juke box tom-toms beat.
   Yellow skirt girl the dust I've seen,
   Red blouse girl the days between
   Breast and breast of a night in town,
   The bugle tears and the lights turned down,

And the talk of you, the talk of you,
The silence and the center of the tents—of
                                        you.

Perhaps Ciardi's work is a little weakened by an occasional
prettiness and a kind of self-regarding charm which shows at its
most obvious in *Goodmorning With Light* where his naming of
himself seems rather too winsome:

Goodmorning, then, with light prepared
Almost a day ago. Light shared
By half the world before it made
This last turn through the window shade,
And, after half a world, involved
John Ciardi in the thing revolved.

But in his poem, *Elegy* (for Kurt Porjescz, missing in action,
April 1, 1945) the slightly tinselly quality is firmly put aside and
a beautiful and moving work is achieved; here are the last
three stanzas, of which there are eight all together:

Clouds had them once, and wreckage mars
                                        them now.
And the same wreckage scatters on your fall.
Spring that amazes more than we allow
Of our dark selves to show, sets equally after
                                        all
On the blind wreck of gland and rationale.

The East runs like a stain across our mouths,
Our engines cry the faltering dark sun down.
And one default of metal breaks our oaths
To cross on sky above a burning town:
On metal's meeting wish is overthrown.

Now only memory keeps its aftermotion.
Goodbye, where no luck serves, nor any word,

Across a swell of sky and cloudy ocean
While April wind and bony bird
Discuss our futures, and have not concurred.

Finally, a brief mention of the only American wartime poet, as far as I am aware, to be influenced, not by the more Augustan modes of Auden, Crowe Ransom and Tate, but by the young British neo-romantics, George Barker and Dylan Thomas. These few lines from *In All the Argosy of Your Bright Hair* are sufficient, I think, to show Dunstan Thompson's debt to Dylan Thomas, though I suppose it is just possible that the American is echoing Hart Crane whom the Welsh poet, in cadence and diction, so often resembles.

Whom I lay down for dead rises up in blood,
Drawn over water after me. His wavering
Footfall echoes from the ocean floor. Blow,
Ye winds, a roundabout. These bully sailors
       flood
My eyes with tears, treacheries. But his voice
       shivering
North in lamentation is all I now know . . . .

And I am pretty sure Thompson had read George Barker when he wrote *Articles of War* of which this is a stanza:

When your ship sailed, O Almirante, my
      Marvel of Peru,
South through archipelagoes of grief I
      followed you,
 Where snakes like pearls coiled undersea
 Equators round drowned albatross
  Of loss—leviathan
As loneliness was Amazon to me:
The viceroy boys, meridian in green,
 Saw my Atlantic cross
Themselves for your imperial Pacific view.

Whatever the origins of Thompson's style it is clearly incapable of dealing effectively with the subject of war. The over decorative, involuted language seems to evade the realities with which it purports to deal, and the frequent invocation of figures and incidents from classical mythology adds to the artificiality. Here are a few lines from another poem and, although drowned sailors are mentioned, one feels no pressure either of real experience or of real feeling behind the verse:

> We are alone with every sailor lost at sea
> Whose drowning is repeated day by day. The
> > sound
> Of bells from buoys mourning sunken ships
> > rings round
> Us, warning away the launch that journeys
> > you and me
> > On last Cytherean trips in spring.
> > There the rocks are where sirens sing
> > Like nightingales of death . . . .

Of course the poet would protest that his lines were not intended to present the physical fact of death: the poem's title, *Largo*, is indicative of its tendency towards the abstract, towards 'the condition of music' and its content is personal, a private statement of love, but I suspect that most readers will find as little evidence of true human feeling towards the person to whom the poem is addressed as there is a sense of its being written in wartime by a serving soldier.

The trouble is that Thompson's poetry is too much intent on being beautiful literature and it seems perversely trivial and narcissistic when the circumstances of its composition are considered. As we have seen, it was possible to write honestly about the war, even in its most brutal aspects, and at the same time tap a vein of lyricism, but this was accomplished only by those poets who were prepared to face the reality, however terrible or ugly or boring, and write with honesty of what they saw and what they felt.

❁

I am aware of the fact that I have made no mention of a number of writers who served with one or other of the US armed forces during the Second World War and who wrote poems from their experience of doing so, men like Stanley Kunitz, William Meredith and Donald Stauffer, all of whom produced work of real merit, but examination of and quotation from their wartime verse would not, I feel, add significantly to the general picture of American war poetry supplied by the authors I have dealt with. What I hope that my brief survey has shown is that the poetic impulse was not inhibited either by the adverse material conditions of service life or by the supremecy of the forces of darkness and destruction which war released, that in the United States, as in Britain, the creative spirit could not be stifled; next that the best poetry of the war, the most truthful and penetrating was written with a respect for that tradition of English verse which is informed by the spirit of Milton's words, 'simple, sensuous and passionate', a poetry which is rooted in the ground of physical experience, suspicious of the abstract and conforming to the disciplines of provenly effective forms.

Robert Graves, in his autobiographical *Goodbye to All That*, writes of Thomas Hardy's words: 'All we can do is write on the old themes in the old styles, but try to do a little better than those who went before us.' This statement has been smiled at by many self-consciously modern, experimental writers and regarded as being conservative, even timid in its lack of adventurousness. But is it really so? If we bear in mind that 'those who went before us' include Shakespeare, Donne, Milton and Pope, to mention only a handful of the giants of the past, to 'try to do a little better' than these is not a timid ambition but one verging on the audacious. However that may be, I feel that the best of the American poets of the Second World War—Kirstein, Jarrell, Simpson and Wilbur—as much as they differ from each other in style and substance, would find themselves in general agreement with Thomas Hardy's counsel as would the best of the British war poets, Douglas, Lewis, and Fuller. Finally, I hope that I have shown that the best poetry of the Second World War written by British and American servicemen need not fear comparison with the generally more highly-regarded work of the 1914–18 poets.

Notes

1. *The New Poetic* by C. K. Stead. London 1964.
2. Middleton Murry—*The Nation and the Athenaeum*. 1921.
3. *The Letters of W. B. Yeats*. Ed. Allan Wade. London 1954.
4. *English Poetry of the First World War* by John H. Johnston. 1964.
5. Blunden has said . . . (in conversation with the author).
6. *Out of Battle* by Jon Silkin. Oxford 1972.
7. *The Home Front. England 1939–45* by Marion Yass. London 1971.
8. *The Whitsun Weddings* by Philip Larkin. London 1964.
9. *Somme and Flanders* by Peter Porter. Penguin Modern Poets 1962.
10. *Collected Poems of Keith Douglas*. Ed. John Waller, G. S. Fraser, and J. C. Hall. London 1966.
11. *Alamein to Zem Zem* by Keith Douglas. London 1966.
12. *Tradition and the Individual Talent* by T. S. Eliot. *The Sacred Wood* London 1920.
13. *Selected Poems of Keith Douglas*. Ed. Ted Hughes. 1964.
14. *The Forties* by Ian Hamilton. *London Magazine*. April 1964.
15. *In the Green Tree*. Letters and short stories by Alun Lewis. Preface by A. L. Rowse. London 1948.
16. *Alun Lewis's Selected Poetry and Prose*. Introduction by Ian Hamilton. London 1966.
17. *Ibid.*
18. *The Forties* by Ian Hamilton. *The London Magazine*. April 1964.
19. *In the Green Tree*.
20. *The Forties* by Ian Hamilton.
21. Letter quoted in the Introduction to *Ha! Ha! Among the Trumpets* (Foreword by Robert Graves). London 1945.
22. *Ibid.*

23. *Ibid.*
24. *Eight Oxford Poets.* Ed. Michael Meyer and Sidney Keyes. 1941.
25. *Collected Poems of Sidney Keyes.* Ed. Michael Meyer. London 1945.
26. (Letter) *Ibid.*
27. *The Forties* by Ian Hamilton. *London Magazine.* April 1964.
28. Quoted in the *Memoir* by Michael Meyer, *Collected Poems of Sidney Keyes.*
29. *The Poetry of War 1939–45.* Ed. Ian Hamilton. London 1965.
30. 'Henry Reed has said. . . .' (in conversation with the author).
31. *Elegies for the Dead in Cyrenaica* by Hamish Henderson. London 1948.
32. *The Poetry of War 1939–45.* Ed. Ian Hamilton. London 1965.
33. *Ibid.*
34. *Ibid.*
35. *The War Poets.* Ed. Oscar Williams. New York 1945.
36. *Ibid.* (prose comment from Eberhart).

Select Bibliography

Poetry Collections

Drummond Allison: *The Yellow Night.* Fortune Press 1944.
Jocelyn Brooke: *December Spring.* Bodley Head 1946.
Norman Cameron: *Work in Hand.* Hogarth Press 1942.
Charles Causley: *Farewell Aggie Weston.* Hand & Flower Press 1951.
   Survivor's Leave. Hand & Flower Press 1953.
   Union Street. Hart-Davis 1960.
Roy Campbell: *Talking Bronco.* Faber 1940.
Herbert Corby: *Hampdens Going Over.* Editions Poetry. London 1945.
   Time in a Blue Prison. Fortune Press 1947.
R. N. Currey: *This Other Planet.* Routledge 1945.
   Indian Landscape. Routledge 1947.
Keith Douglas: *Selected Poems.* Ed. Ted Hughes, Faber 1964.
   Collected Poems. Ed. Waller, Fraser and Hall, Faber 1966.
Richard Eberhart: *Collected Poems* 1930–1960. Chatto & Windus
   1960.
Roy Fuller: *The Middle of a War.* Hogarth Press 1942.
   A Lost Season. Hogarth Press 1944.
   Collected Poems. Andre Deutsch 1962.
Anthony Hecht: *The Hard Hours.* O.U.P. 1967.
Hamish Henderson: *Elegies for the Dead in Cyrenaica.* Lehmann 1948.
Randall Jarrell: *The Complete Poems.* Faber 1971.
Sidney Keyes: *The Iron Laurel.* Routledge 1942.
   The Cruel Solstice. Routledge 1943.
   Collected Poems. Routledge 1945.
Lincoln Kirstein: *Rhymes and More Rhymes of a PFC.* New Directions
   1966.

Alun Lewis: *Raiders' Dawn*. Allen & Unwin 1942.

  Ha! Ha! Among the Trumpets. Allen & Unwin 1944.

John Manifold: *Selected Verse*. Dennis Dobson 1948.

Howard Nemerov: *The Image and the Law*. Holy, N.Y., 1947.

  New and Selected Poems. University of Chicago 1960.

  Five American Poets. Ed. Gunn & Hughes, Faber 1963.

F. T. Prince: *Soldiers Bathing*. Fortune Press 1954.

  The Doors of Stone. Hart-Davis 1963.

Henry Reed: *A Map of Verona*. Cape 1946.

Alan Ross: *The Derelict Day*.

  Something of the Sea. Verschoyle 1954.

  To Whom it may Concern. Hamish Hamilton 1958.

  Poems 1942–67. Eyre & Spottiswoode 1967.

  Open Sea. London Magazine Editions, 1975.

Karl Shapiro: *Person, Place and Thing*. Secker & Warburg 1944.

  V-Letter. Secker & Warburg 1945.

Louis Simpson: *Selected Poems*. O.U.P. 1966.

  Five American Poets. Ed. Gunn & Hughes, Faber 1963.

Richard Wilbur: *Poems 1943–1956*. Faber 1957.

Anthologies

Poetry

Ronald Blythe ed. *Components of the Scene* (1966).
Brian Gardner: *The Terrible Rain* (1966).
Ian Hamilton: *The Poetry of War 1939–45* (1965).
John Lehmann: *Poems from New Writing* (1946).
Robin Skelton: *Poetry of the Forties* (1968).
Oscar Williams: *The War Poets* (N.Y. 1945).

Prose

R. N. Currey: *Poets of the 1939–1945 War* (1960).
Mildred Davidson: *The Poetry is in the Pity* (1972).
Keith Douglas: *Alamein to Zem Zem* (1946).
Desmond Graham: *Keith Douglas, a Biography* (1974).
Alun Lewis: *In the Green Tree* (1948).
Stephen Spender: *Poetry Since 1939* (1946).
Louis Simpson: *Air with Armed Men* (1972).

Index

COLLEGE OF MARIN

3 2555 00121358 1

DATE DUE